# THE RESILIENT HUSBAND

## THE CONFIDENT MAN'S GUIDE TO REBUILDING TRUST, DEEPENING LOVE, AND LEADING WITH STRENGTH

### SVEN MASTERSON

SVEN
MASTERSON
MENTOR FOR MEN

# COPYRIGHT

**Sven Masterson, LLC**
320 Gold Ave. SW Ste. 620
Albuquerque, NM 87102 USA

**First Edition**

**Library of Congress Cataloging-in-Publication Data**

**Names:** Sven Masterson, author.

**Title:** *The Resilient Husband:* The Confident Man's Guide to Rebuilding Trust, Deepening Love, and Leading with Strength / Sven Masterson

**Description:** First Edition. | Albuquerque: Sven Masterson, LLC, 2024. | Includes bibliographical references.

**Identifiers:**

- *(ebook)* ISBN 979-8-9921098-5-6

- *(paperback)* ISBN 979-8-9921098-6-3

**Subjects:** LCSH: Marriage—Psychological aspects. | Interpersonal relations. | Self-help. |

**BISAC:** FAMILY & RELATIONSHIPS / Marriage & Long-Term Relationships. | SELF-HELP / Personal Growth / Success.

**Classification:** LCC HQXXXX .M37 2024 | DDC 306.8—dc23

Cover design by Sven Masterson

Published by Sven Masterson, LLC

**First Printing, 2025**

# DEDICATION

*For my dad —*
*You didn't have the words or tools to teach me these things, but you gave*
*me something just as valuable.*
*Perseverance when things felt impossible.*
*Tenacity when the weight was too much.*
*Patience when there were no easy answers.*
*You carried burdens you never got to set down.*
*You fought battles no one saw. Still are.*
*And you kept going. Still are.*

*Those attributes saved my life–and marriage, Dad. Thank you!*

*I've had the privilege of finding the tools you didn't have — but I stand on*
*the foundation you built.*
*This book is for men like <u>us</u>.*

# CONTENTS

# INTRODUCTION
## WHY THIS BOOK EXISTS

## THE MANSION AND ROOMS: A NEW WAY TO SEE YOUR MARRIAGE

A few years ago, I wrote an article titled *"Why Your Wife Keeps Bringing Up the Past, Won't Let It Go, and What You Can Do About It."* It was one of many pieces I had written about relationships, but something about this one was different. It didn't just get more attention—it exploded (compared to my other writing).

The traffic to that article wasn't just a little higher than my other writings; it was hundreds of times greater. Men weren't just reading it—they were searching for it over and over again. The comments, emails, and coaching inquiries that followed all had a common theme:

*"This is exactly what I've been struggling with. Why does she keep bringing up the past?"*

That level of interest told me something important. It wasn't just an isolated frustration—it was a widespread, nearly universal pain point for men in long-term relationships.

And I understood why.

Because I had been there too.

## THE FRUSTRATION OF THE "SAME OLD ARGUMENTS"

For years in my own marriage, I felt like my wife and I were trapped in a frustrating loop.

We would be doing fine—or at least I *thought* we were—and then, out of nowhere, she would bring up something from months or even years ago. Something I thought was already resolved.

In my mind, these old arguments were dead issues. In hers, they were very much alive. She didn't just bring up the past, either, but did so with a staggering amount of details, none of which I remembered. It often felt like what I imagine an FBI interrogation might feel like.

And every time it happened, I felt an immediate mix of frustration, confusion, and sometimes even anger.

- *Why are we talking about this again?*
- *Haven't we already been through this?*
- *Why can't she just let it go and move forward?*

I wanted to get past it so we could move on. But no matter what I tried—explaining my point of view, apologizing (again), imploring her to move on, or trying to shut the conversation down—it didn't work.

She kept bringing it up. Over and over again.

And because I didn't understand why, I assumed it meant one of two things:

1. She was holding onto a grudge and refusing to move on.
2. There was something deeply wrong with our relationship.

Neither of those thoughts made me feel hopeful about the future.

But here's what I didn't realize at the time:

I wasn't actually stuck in a loop of the same argument.

I was stuck in a relationship *mansion* I didn't understand.

## WHAT IS THE MANSION?

If you've ever walked through an old, sprawling house, you know the feeling—hallways that twist and turn, doors that lead to unexpected places, and rooms that hold history you may not fully understand.

Your marriage is like that house.

Every meaningful experience, every conversation, every moment of connection or conflict exists within it. Some rooms are filled with warmth, love, and intimacy. Others hold pain, unresolved tension, or unmet needs. Some doors are wide open, easy to step into. Others have been shut—locked away, but never forgotten.

I didn't know it yet, but my wife wasn't trying to rehash old fights just to punish me.

She was trying to take me into a room in our marriage's mansion —a place where something had been left unresolved, unfinished, or unhealed.

The problem was that I had never been taught how to navigate the hallways, rooms, and closets of this mansion.

Like many men, my natural instinct was to keep moving forward —to build the next room, focus on the next thing, and assume that anything from the past should stay in the past.

But I learned that's not how women experience long-term relationships.

Women tend to revisit old rooms—not because they want to dwell on the past, but because those rooms contain unfinished emotional business that will not go away on their own.

When I ignored those rooms or refused to enter them with her, the past wasn't forgotten. It meant the mansion was slowly becoming *haunted*.

Doors were shutting. Unfinished emotions were festering. And over time, the unaddressed pain created more distance between us.

## WHY THIS BOOK USES THE MANSION AS A GUIDE

If you're reading this book, it's probably because you've felt exactly what I felt.

- You're frustrated by hearing about the past—again.
- You feel like no matter what you do, she doesn't seem to move on.
- You're tired of trying to endlessly explain yourself.
- You are frustrated that you don't recall what you felt and thought back then, even though she wants to know more.
- You worry that your whole relationship might be in trouble if she keeps bringing up old hurts.

I get it. This book isn't here to tell you that you've failed, that you're broken, or that your instincts as a man are flawed. I know men, and I know that's not true. Men are capable, driven, and full of potential—but too many are navigating relationships without a clear map.

That's what this book is here to give you—a way forward that actually works.

Once I began to see my marriage as a mansion with many rooms —and, more importantly, why my wife wanted to explore those old rooms—everything changed.

- Instead of seeing my wife's emotions as problems that needed to be fixed, I started seeing them as doors that needed to be opened.
- Instead of trying to avoid old rooms, I learned how to enter them with confidence and presence.
- Instead of losing myself in the process, I found that by staying fully me, I could create more connection than ever before.

And that's what I want for you, too.

This book will show you:

- Why your wife keeps bringing up the past (and why it's not what you think).
- Why avoiding old arguments doesn't create peace—it creates distance.
- How to stop feeling powerless in emotional conversations and show up with confidence.
- How to move through your marriage's mansion without losing yourself.

Your marriage isn't permanently broken.
You just need the right map.
Let's get started.

# WHO THIS BOOK IS FOR
## AND AN INVITATION TO THOSE WHO LOVE THEM

## WHO THIS BOOK IS FOR (AND WHO IT MIGHT STILL HELP)

This book is written for men in long-term, committed, monogamous relationships—specifically husbands who want to confidently lead their marriage, deepen trust, and create lasting connection.

As a men's coach and mentor, I work directly with men in this context every day. I've seen these principles transform marriages—helping men move from frustration, distance, and resentment to clarity, connection, and leadership.

## BUT WHAT ABOUT OTHER RELATIONSHIPS?

If you're in a long-term, committed relationship but not married, or even if you're a woman hoping to understand the struggles your husband faces—you may still find this book valuable. Many of the dynamics I describe are universal to relationships, especially where trust, communication, and emotional leadership are concerned.

## HOWEVER, I WANT TO BE CLEAR: I STAY IN MY LANE.

I believe, wholeheartedly, that anyone who wants to understand what a woman wants and needs in a romantic relationship will gain valuable insights from this book. However, I don't make claims about what I haven't personally seen work repeatedly within my relationships and the men I've coached. While the insights in this book are grounded in universal principles of trust, leadership, and emotional connection, my focus has always been on helping men lead in committed, heterosexual relationships. That's where I've seen the most success, the most transformation, and the most lasting impact.

If that's your situation, I can confidently tell you that this book will still help you. If not, you're still welcome here, and I encourage you to explore these ideas for yourself.

## THE UNSUNG ADVOCATES: WHY WIVES AND PARTNERS OFTEN REFER ME THE MOST

One of the most surprising things I've learned in my years of coaching men is this: My biggest source of personal referrals isn't men—*it's their wives and partners.*

It's not that the men I work with don't appreciate the transformation they experience—they do. In fact, most of them tell me that what they've learned feels like a secret weapon for building trust, leadership, and deep emotional connection in their marriage. But here's the funny thing…

They rarely want to tell their friends about it. They're a little *too* protective of it at times!

Some of that is just how men operate. We tend to be private about anything that might make us seem like we need help. Many men also feel a little sheepish about admitting they were struggling in their relationship in the first place. So they quietly take what they've learned, apply it, and enjoy the results—but they're not always quick to shout from the rooftops about how they got there.

Their wives, though? They talk–and I'm glad they do because men *need* this.

I can't tell you how many times I've had a new client reach out because his wife sent him my website, an article, or a video and said,

*"You need to check this guy out."*

Or how often I get messages from women asking, *"How can I get my husband to contact you for mentoring?"*

Women see the shifts in their men, feel the difference in their marriages, and naturally want other women to experience the same thing. Because women talk about relationships far more than men do, they become the ones who spread the word.

This is important to mention because if you're a woman reading this book, you might be wondering:

*"How do I get my husband to read this without making him feel like he's failing or needs to be 'fixed'?"*

Below, I'll give you a few guiding principles for inviting him into this without triggering defensiveness, shame, or resistance. The truth is, most husbands really want a great marriage—they just need a way that feels natural, safe, and aligned with their *strengths*.

## AN INVITATION TO WOMEN READING THIS BOOK

If you're a woman reading this book, it likely means you deeply care about your relationship and are searching for ways to bridge the gap between you and your husband.

First of all, I see you. I know how painful it can be when you feel like you're speaking a different language than the man you love, when emotional conversations feel like battles instead of bridges, and when it doesn't seem to land, no matter how much you try to explain what you need.

If you're hoping your husband will read this book, you're not alone. Many women have found these insights helpful for under-standing their husbands—and many have successfully invited their husbands into this understanding and work. But if you've ever tried to hand a book to a man and been met with resistance, you already know that *how* you introduce it matters.

Here are a few key principles to keep in mind if you'd like to invite your husband to read this book without triggering defensiveness or resistance:

### Speak to his strength, not his shortcomings.

As men, we don't respond well to being told we're failing or that we "need help." Instead of saying, *"You really need to read this,"* try something like, *"I know how much you care about me/us, and I think you'd really appreciate the perspective in this book. They'd bring out your best!"* We're more likely to lean in when we feel like you're recognizing our efforts rather than criticizing us.

### Express what it would provide for you.

Instead of focusing on what we *need* to do, share what reading this book would *give you* emotionally. Saying something like, *"I'd feel so much more understood if we could talk about some of the ideas in this book together,"* invites us into connection rather than making us feel obligated.

### Avoid presenting it as a demand.

Men love and strive for freedom. If reading a book feels like another "chore" or "assignment," we will likely resist it–and you. Instead, you might say, *"I read something in here that really spoke to me, and I'd love to hear your thoughts on it,"* which makes it about curiosity and shared conversation rather than a task.

### Recognize that he might process differently.

Most of us, as men, aren't used to approaching relationship struggles through books or introspection. If we hesitate, remind us that this what you're inviting us into isn't about blame or forcing emotional conversations—it's about practical, real-world insights that can make life *easier* for both of us.

Ultimately, the best way to encourage us as men to engage with an idea is to foster an environment where we feel respected, appreciated, and invited rather than criticized, pressured, or shamed.

Hopefully, you can see that we ultimately want the same things our wives do.

## FINAL THOUGHTS

At the end of the day, my goal with this book is simple: **to help good men become stronger, more confident, and more capable of leading their relationships toward trust, connection, and lasting love.**

If you're a man reading this book, you're in the right place.

If you're a woman reading this book, I hope it gives you valuable insight into your husband's experience—and, if he's open to it, a path forward you can walk together.

Wherever you are in your journey, I'm honored to walk alongside you.

Now, let's get started.

# PROLOGUE
## LEADING WITH STRENGTH, NOT CONTROL

W hen I first started learning what it really meant to lead in marriage, I didn't have all the answers (and I still don't). In fact, I had a lot of the wrong ones. Like many men, I assumed that if I worked hard, provided, and stayed committed, that should be enough. But like many men also discover, my marriage didn't thrive just because I got up and went to work every day and generally played nice—it required me to step into real leadership, emotional strength, and deep personal ownership.

I've been married for 30 years at this writing, and I've had the opportunity to apply, test, and refine these principles in real life. I haven't just studied marriage or coached men on these topics—I've lived them through both the hardest moments of marriage and the deeply fulfilling rewards that come from stepping into leadership.

More than that, I've seen these principles work beyond just my own marriage. My wife, Zelda, and I have raised six kids, three of whom are now entering their relationships and future marriages, and three who will do so sooner than I'd sometimes like. All of them have seen these concepts modeled in real life, and they're already implementing them in their own ways as they step into adulthood. I am not just handing down theories—but what we have been watching the next generation embrace and apply to leading in love, trust, and deep connection. We're proud of the results.

## FOR THE CRITICS: NO, THIS ISN'T WEAK, AND NO, IT DOESN'T KILL ATTRACTION

I know there will be men who scoff at this and think, "This is weak. This kind of 'emotional leadership' just turns men into docile, sexless pushovers."

Let me be clear: That's not what happened in our marriage. The leadership you'll read about has and continues to create a better life and marriage than I ever imagined—the ones such voices bemoan as impossible and unobtainable.

The men who believe that leadership in marriage means control, dominance, or emotional distance are playing a boyish, shallow game based on hurt and pain, not strength. They think they have to be cold and guarded to keep a woman's attraction or that emotions are inherently feminine and weak.

But in my experience? A man who can lead with strength, confidence, and emotional security doesn't lose attraction—he amplifies it.

- My wife respects me—not because I demand it, but because I cherish and respect her and lead with conviction and self-trust.
- Our relationship is full of intimacy and deep connection—not because I walk around reminding her that I'm an "alpha male" or being hyper-focused on my testosterone levels, fitness PRs, the right pickup tactics, and the right personal grooming techniques but because I'm unshakable in my sense of self-worth and consistent in the presence I offer to her.
- I don't chase validation, I don't walk on eggshells, and I don't need her approval to be secure in who I am.

If that sounds like weakness to some men, then I'd suggest they don't understand real strength–or that it's not a kind of strength I need or want. They also shouldn't read this book.

What I teach in this book isn't about becoming a neutered "nice guy" or a passive husband who spends his life in resentful servitude, catering to his wife's every whim. It isn't built upon a "happy wife, happy life" philosophy. It's about being the kind of man who creates an unshakable marriage—not through force but through authentic leadership and inspiring devotion instead of demanding fealty.

And if you don't believe that's possible? Stick with me. By the time you finish this book, you'll either see the truth in it, or you'll still be chasing the same exhausting ego-driven race to the bottom.

The choice is yours.

## A REALITY CHECK FOR MEN WHO WANT MORE THAN A TEMPORARY FIX

There are many loud voices out there telling men how to "handle" women, how to "win" in relationships, and how to "take back power." I get it–these popular expressions are great for selling books and gaining views, likes, and comments.

But here's what I want you to think about for a second:

- What is the substance of the men behind those messages?
- Are they actually building deeply connected, long-term relationships?
- Are they leading marriages that thrive in every way— emotionally, sexually, and relationally?
- Are they leaving a legacy of strength, wisdom, and love for their children to follow?

Or... are they just selling anger, manipulation, and short-term tactics—while their own relationships tend to crash and burn in the face of adversity?

The approach in this book isn't about getting one over on someone, taking power from them, or making them submit.

- Though it sometimes involves tearing down ideas and habits that don't work, it does so to create something new, not toxic relational fallout, and without tearing down others, including most of all your wife or partner.
- It doesn't require her to be small, so you can be great.
- It doesn't require you to "win" by making her or anyone else a loser.
- It doesn't teach you to manipulate or out-game your wife.

Because if your version of strength requires someone else to be weaker, it's not real strength.

**That's not leadership.
That's insecurity wearing a mask.**

I don't teach men how to gain the upper hand. I teach men how to become the kind of men who naturally create connection, respect, trust, and attraction—not by force or control but by becoming unshakable and leading in a way that inspires love to thrive.

And here's the hardest and most freeing truth you'll find in this book:

- When you become that kind of man, everything else follows.
- Respect follows. Connection follows. Attraction follows.

Because the *kind of man* you become determines the *kind of marriage* you have.

I know that might challenge some deeply held beliefs.

And that's a good thing. Don't read this book if you aren't ready to be challenged.

If you feel a gut punch reading this, try to move past seeing it as shame and see it instead as an opportunity. That's your wake-up call to step into something bigger, stronger, and better than the path you've been on.

So if you're ready to actually lead—not just in a way that gets you through another year of marriage, but in a way that makes your wife feel safe, seen, and drawn to you in a way you haven't felt in years—then let's go.

Because I promise you this:

This *isn't* about playing a game.

This *isn't* about pretending to be someone you're not.

This *isn't* about controlling or dominating your wife.

This *isn't* about techniques to make her shut up.

This *is* about becoming a man who trusts himself so deeply and humbly that she can trust you, too.

And when you do that... the kind of marriage you want naturally follows.

I've lived this and have helped many men do the same.

What you'll read in this book will get you started.

# BEFORE YOU DIVE IN: A WORD ABOUT HOW THIS BOOK MIGHT HIT YOU

## A NOTE FROM SVEN

If you're anything like me, you don't read books like this just for fun.

You're here because something in your life—probably your marriage—isn't where you want it to be. Maybe you feel stuck, frustrated, or like you've tried everything, and nothing has worked.

That means, as you read this book, you might have moments where something hits you hard.

Some ideas might resonate instantly—lighting you up with possibility and a sense of, *"Finally, this makes sense."*

Other ideas might make you uncomfortable. You might feel the urge to skim past certain parts, dismiss something outright, or put the book down and tell yourself, *"Yeah, I don't need this part."*

I say that because **that's exactly what I used to do.**

For years, I consumed books, podcasts, and videos, gathering all kinds of knowledge—without actually letting it change me. Looking back, I can see that it wasn't because I was lazy or unwilling. It was because, deep down, I didn't want to look at certain things too closely.

To be transparent–I avoided, minimized, and justified things— not because I was incapable of change, but because I didn't want to feel the discomfort of facing certain truths.

And if that happens to you as you read, I want you to recognize it for what it is: **a completely normal reaction.**

## PUSH THROUGH THE RIGHT KIND OF DISCOMFORT

Now, let me be clear: **Not every message is for every man at every time.**

There may be parts of this book that truly don't apply to you or that aren't relevant to your situation right now. That's fine.

But there's a difference between skipping something because it's *irrelevant* and skipping something because it makes you *uncomfortable.*

> **Discomfort isn't a sign that something is *wrong.***
> **It's often a sign that something is *important.***

So, as you read, if you feel resistance, pause. Sit with it. Ask yourself, *"What about this is making me uncomfortable? What if this is true? And if it is, what would that mean for me?"*

This book isn't here to tell you that you've been doing everything wrong. Quite the contrary! I think the best about you! It's here to give you a new map that works.

The men who get the most out of this book aren't the ones who read it the fastest. They're the ones who take their time, wrestle with the ideas, and keep going—even when it gets uncomfortable.

So, as you read, pay attention to what lands and what you feel resistance to. Both will tell you something valuable.

Alright—let's get started.

# PART ONE
# HOW THE MANSION GETS HAUNTED

## WHY YOUR MARRIAGE FEELS LIKE IT'S SLIPPING AWAY

.

# ONE
# THE MANSION OF LOVE
## WHY MARRIAGE CHANGES OVER TIME

---

*Love doesn't die a natural death. It dies because we don't know how to replenish its source.*

— Anaïs Nin

---

## EVERY MARRIAGE BEGINS IN A MANSION OF OPEN DOORS

When I first fell in love, it felt like stepping into a grand mansion I had never seen before. Maybe you felt the same.

At first, everything was open, new, and unexplored. Every hallway led to a new adventure, every room held a new discovery, and every moment together felt like a journey into something incredible.

We walked hand in hand, exploring every corner of this vast space together.

- There was a room for laughter, where we shared effortless joy and inside jokes.

- There was a room for affection, where physical connection came naturally, without overthinking.
- There was a room for deep conversations, where we stayed up late, sharing dreams and secrets, hungry to know each other more.

Everywhere we turned, there was excitement, possibility, acceptance, and connection. For a while, it felt like this was always the case.

The doors were open. The light poured in. We could move freely from one room to another, basking in the warmth of our relationship.

But at some point, something changed.

## HOW SOME ROOMS BEGIN TO SHUT

Maybe it happened slowly, so gradually that we didn't even notice.

Maybe there was a moment—a fight, a misunderstanding, a betrayal of trust—where something in the mansion shifted.

A door, once open, now creaked on its hinges.

At first, we thought, *It's fine. We'll get back to that room later.*

But then, it happened again.

Another door quietly shut.

- Maybe it was the Room of Playfulness, where we used to joke and tease each other, but now every joke seems to land wrong.
- Maybe it was the Room of Spontaneous Affection, where physical touch used to be easy but now feels like an unspoken negotiation.
- Maybe it was the Room of Emotional Safety, where she once opened up freely but now hesitates, withholding parts of herself.

At first, it didn't seem like a big deal. After all, the mansion was still huge. There were plenty of other rooms where we still felt connected.

So we kept moving forward, focusing on building new rooms—a home, a career, children, responsibilities.

And we assumed that the old rooms would stay in the past.

After all, why go back? Why revisit a room that's already been closed?

But then, something unsettling happened.

She started leading me back to those rooms.

She brought up things I thought were long behind us.

She asked me to step into spaces I had avoided.

And when I hesitated—when I resisted opening that door—she got upset.

I felt like she was dragging me backward. Like she was fixated on things that should have been left alone.

It was frustrating. It was exhausting. And at some point, I started wondering:

*"Why does she keep bringing up the past?"*

## WHY MEN AND WOMEN EXPERIENCE THE MANSION DIFFERENTLY

At first, I thought the answer was obvious:

Because she wouldn't let things go.

But that assumption turned out to be dead wrong.

What I didn't understand—what many of us don't understand—is that men and women experience the mansion in completely different ways.

### Men See Progress as Forward Motion

For me, progress has always been about building. *Creating.* Moving *forward.*

When we bought our homestead in the mountains of Pennsylvania, I went into full-on builder mode.

- I built a barn.
- Then, a goat barn.
- Then, a woodshed.

- Then, a duck house.
- Then, a chicken coop.
- Then, a turkey enclosure.
- Then, I built a warren (that is a place where one raises rabbits. I had to look that up!).
- Then, I built gardens, orchards, and bee hives.

I remodeled. I repaired. I renewed.

As the old saying goes... *I was busier than a one-legged man in a butt-kicking contest.*

And many evenings, I'd come inside sweaty, exhausted, thirsty, and stinking like hard work, diesel fuel, and 2-stroke fumes.

I wanted Zelda to express her appreciation for my hard work and effort, but instead, she would say something like, *"Honey! When are you going to install that missing base trim in the hallway and those receptacle covers in our room?"*

And I would be... *incredulous.*

*"Are you kidding me?"*

*"Did she really just say that?"*

*"Do you not see everything I'm doing, woman?!"*

*"Can't you appreciate all the big things I've built?"*

I felt insulted, overlooked, unappreciated, and disrespected in those moments.

At the time, I thought she was nitpicking. I thought she just didn't see how much I was doing. I thought I had a nasty, defective, and adversarial wife and that maybe I needed a new one.

But now, I know I was experiencing a two-fold problem:

1. Those feelings—of being overlooked, unappreciated, and disrespected—already existed *inside* me. No matter what I thought otherwise, they had nothing to do with her. Her words were just triggering an opportunity for me to notice them and, like a mirror, showed me what I needed to see, even if it was painful to look at.
2. I misunderstood how women see progress—not as forward motion but as completion.

## Women See Progress as Completion

Where I saw progress as expanding *outward, onwards,* and *forward,* my wife saw progress as bringing things to *completion.* Wince.

I enjoy creating new spaces. She enjoys filling them with love–and sometimes, lots of little knickknacks I don't quite understand.

- I book the vacations. She makes sure every detail is planned and perfect.
- I'm excited about *where* we're going. *Her? She's excited about what outfits* she will wear while we're there. I'm thinking about the sights we'll see in Dublin; she's thinking about which scarves and earrings will look best on the streets of Dublin.
- I build the new spaces. She wants to choose the colors and fill them with furniture, decor, and warmth.
- I start the big projects. She notices the little things that make them feel complete–and often, the details I miss or, frankly–don't care that much about.

This is how we've complemented each other in our marriage.

But I didn't see it that way for the first twenty years.

For two decades, I felt like she was pointing out my shortcomings while I was out there making the important stuff happen. It felt adversarial, critical, unkind, and mean-spirited.

After years of reflection, I see that she wasn't intentionally criticizing me—she was doing what she does best: trying to fill and complete the spaces I was creating.

When I resisted—when I became defensive, angry, or shut down—I rejected a fundamental part of our partnership's design.

I didn't know that at the time.

I just thought she was ungrateful.

And that belief kept us stuck in the same exhausting loop for years.

But even once I began to understand this fundamental difference, one question still gnawed at me:

*"If she's really just trying to reconnect, why does it feel like she's attacking me?"*

At first, I didn't have a good answer. It still *felt* like criticism and triggered frustration, defensiveness, and resentment.

But the more I stepped back and looked at our dynamic, the more I realized something important:

She wasn't trying to take something from me. She was trying to create something *with* me.

What I had seen as *corrections* were actually invitations—her way of saying, *"This space isn't complete yet. Can we finish it together?"*

It was never about tearing down what I had built. It was about wanting to stand in it *with* me, fully, without unspoken tension or unfinished business lingering in the air.

And that changed everything.

## MAIN TAKEAWAY: LOVE STARTS OPEN—BUT IT CAN'T STAY THAT WAY WITHOUT UNDERSTANDING

Every marriage begins in a place of warmth, excitement, and deep connection. The mansion is open and full of possibilities. In those early days, everything feels effortless—every room is inviting, every conversation is filled with curiosity, and every moment together feels expansive.

But over time, something shifts.

It's not that love disappears—it's that *we don't always know how to sustain it.*

Many of us mistakenly think our wives are dragging us *backward* when she brings up the past. In reality, she's trying to *complete something*, to restore connection in a way that makes sense to her.

When we fail to recognize this, we resist her invitations to closeness, misinterpret her needs as criticism, and assume the past should stay in the past, not realizing that *for her, it never fully left.*

But love isn't about moving *on*—it's about moving *through*– together.

The connection we felt in the beginning didn't just happen—it was created. And if we don't continue creating it, we wake up one day feeling like something is missing.

The challenge is not just to build—but to build *with* her in a way that honors both perspectives.

If we can do that, we don't just keep the doors open—we create a relationship that feels alive, evolving, and deeply fulfilling.

## NEXT UP: TWO DIFFERENT MAPS OF THE MANSION

Now that we understand how rooms get shut, we need to go deeper into why men and women navigate the mansion so differently.

Because if you've ever felt like your wife's emotions don't make sense…

Or like you're constantly being pulled back into rooms you'd rather avoid…

…then you're about to see why this happens—and what to do about it.

Let's move forward.

# TWO
# TWO DIFFERENT MAPS OF THE MANSION

## WHY MEN AND WOMEN EXPERIENCE THE SAME RELATIONSHIP IN COMPLETELY DIFFERENT WAYS

*Men marry women with the hope they will never change. Women marry men with the hope they will change. Invariably they are both disappointed.*

— Albert Einstein

## WHY YOU AND YOUR WIFE NAVIGATE THE SAME MANSION IN COMPLETELY DIFFERENT WAYS

By now, we've seen how the mansion of marriage changes over time.

At first, every room is open—full of light, connection, and possibility. We move freely, exploring it all together.

But as the years pass and wounds accumulate—both big and small—some doors begin to close. Some rooms become haunted.

And suddenly, we find ourselves in a strange place: We're both in the same house, but we're experiencing it completely differently.

She keeps leading us back to rooms we thought were closed.

We keep trying to move forward, building new rooms instead of revisiting old ones.

And this fundamental difference—how men and women navigate the mansion—is at the heart of why so many couples feel stuck, frustrated, and disconnected.

The good news?

Neither of us is doing it *wrong*.

But if we don't understand this difference, we'll keep misinterpreting her actions, and she'll keep feeling unseen and misunderstood.

This chapter is about making that invisible difference visible—so that instead of feeling like we're living with a stranger, we can finally see the mansion through each other's eyes.

## HOW MEN AND WOMEN NAVIGATE THE MANSION DIFFERENTLY

### Men's Map: The Forward-Building Path

For most of us as men, life—and, by extension, relationships—follows a progress-based map.

We naturally want to move forward and *expand*.

We see relationships as something that's built over time, much like constructing a house:

- When we fall in love, we think, *Great! Let's build something amazing together.*
- When conflict happens, we think, *Let's resolve this quickly so we can move on.*
- When our partner is upset, we think, *What's the fastest way to fix this so things feel normal again?*

To us, progress means movement.

In my natural state, if an argument is over, it's over.

Yesterday. I seriously have to focus in order to remember it (maybe that's age?).

If an apology has been given, I assume the issue is closed.

If I am working hard, staying faithful, and being responsible, I assume the relationship is secure.

And I assume that my wife is on the same path I am.

So when Zelda brings up something from six months ago, it doesn't make sense to me.

To me, that would be like walking into a room we finished building long ago, staring at a single crooked picture frame, and refusing to leave until it's fixed.

My instinct is to say:

- *Why are we back here?*
- *Why does this still matter?*
- *Can we just move forward?*

It's not that I don't care.

It's that I don't realize she's following a completely different map to the mansion of our relationship.

### Women's Map: The Revisiting & Completion Path

Women, generally speaking, don't experience relationships as a linear, progress-based path.

Instead, they experience relationships in cycles, patterns, and emotional loops.

Where we see forward movement, they see interconnection.

For them, emotions and experiences don't exist in isolated moments—they weave together, creating an ongoing narrative.

And in their mind, everything that has happened is still shaping what is happening now.

This is why women often revisit past moments—not because they want to dwell on them, but because they need to feel complete before they can fully move forward.

(*Maybe this is why, when Zelda or one of my daughters tells me a story, I feel like I need a giant whiteboard to keep track of all the threads?*)

## COMPLETION BEFORE PROGRESS

To her, you *can't* just build new rooms on top of unresolved ones, just like she *can't* sit down at the table with unfinished business.

- If something from two years ago still lingers, it doesn't matter that we've moved on in our minds.
- If an emotional wound wasn't fully acknowledged, it doesn't matter that we apologized once.
- If she still feels unheard or unseen about something, it doesn't matter that it happened a long time ago.

She isn't trying to *go backward.*

She's trying to complete the past so it stops disrupting the present. To her, it's all interconnected.

She isn't holding a grudge.

She's holding onto an open loop. And if there's one thing I've learned in three decades of marriage—my wife hates open loops of any kind.

To her, it isn't just about an argument that happened months ago.

It's about whether she feels fully emotionally safe, connected, and understood right now.

For her, *Emotional Safety = Minimal Open Loops.*

And if something unresolved from the past is still affecting her ability to feel that way today, then that room isn't closed for her—no matter how much time has passed.

## WHY THIS DIFFERENCE CREATES CONFLICT

Let's put these two maps side by side:

| Men's Map (Progress-Oriented) | Women's Map (Completion-Oriented) |
|---|---|
| "The past should stay in the past." | "The past is still shaping the present." |
| "We already talked about this." | "I still don't feel fully understood." |
| "Why bring this up now?" | "Because it's still affecting me now." |
| "If you love me, move forward with me." | "If you love me, come back and make sure I feel safe." |

When I didn't understand this difference, I assumed she was bringing up the past to criticize me.

When she didn't understand this difference, she assumed I avoided the past because I didn't care.

And this misalignment created a repeating cycle of frustration:

1. She brought up an unresolved hurt.
2. I'd feel like she was dragging us backward.
3. I shut down, avoided the topic, or get defensive.
4. She felt dismissed and alone in her feelings.
5. The issue didn't actually get resolved—it just got buried.

And then, a few months later, it came up again.

Not because she *couldn't let it go.*

But because it was never actually settled.

## THE JUDGMENT TRAP: SEEING DIFFERENCES AS FLAWS

But there was something even deeper happening here.

It's not just different ways of moving through the mansion.

It was judgment.

Most of us, whether we realize it or not, judge the way our wives process emotion.

- We see her revisiting the past as *dwelling.*

- We see her emotional cycles as *irrational.*
- We see her desire for closure as *unnecessary.*

And because it doesn't match our way of thinking, we dismiss it. And to be fair, women do the same thing.

- They see our desire to move forward as *emotional avoidance.*
- They see our lack of emotional expression as *disconnection.*
- They assume that if we're not revisiting something, it must mean we *don't care.*

And the more we judge each other's maps, the more we create disconnection and distance.

Because instead of respecting the differences, we start seeing them as flaws.

We will revisit this more deeply in a chapter coming up.

## THE KEY: LEARNING TO RESPECT EACH OTHER'S MAPS

If you take nothing else from this chapter, remember this:

Neither of us is *wrong.*

- We're not wrong for wanting to move forward.
- She's not wrong for wanting to make sure the past is fully healed before doing so.

The problem isn't that we're too *different.*

The problem is that we judge those differences as *defects.*

And when we do that, we both feel resentful, misunderstood, and *alone.*

## YOUR WIFE'S EMOTIONAL PROCESS ISN'T A PROBLEM—IT'S AN OPPORTUNITY

Here's something men don't quickly realize:

Her emotional process isn't just something we must tolerate—it's an opportunity.

When we feel triggered by her emotions...

When we find ourselves getting defensive...

When we feel the urge to shut down or avoid a conversation...

It's not just about *her*.

It's about *us*.

The places where we struggle to meet her emotionally are often the same places where we struggle to meet *ourselves*.

And if we can learn to meet ourselves in those places, something powerful happens:

We don't just get a happier marriage.

We become stronger, more unshakable men.

## MAIN TAKEAWAY: YOU'RE NOT TRULY STUCK—YOU'RE SPEAKING DIFFERENT LANGUAGES

Men and women navigate relationships differently, but neither is wrong. Men move forward by building; women move forward by completing. When your wife brings up the past, she's not dragging you backward—she's trying to clear unfinished business so it stops affecting the present.

The biggest mistake we men make is assuming she's holding a grudge when, in reality, she's holding onto an open loop that needs to be closed. If we see her revisiting past pain as an attack, we'll resist. But if we see it as an invitation to strengthen trust and connection, everything changes.

The goal isn't to fix her emotions or make her more like us—it's to respect each other's maps and move through the mansion together.

## NEXT UP: HOW THE MANSION BECOMES HAUNTED

Unresolved emotions don't simply vanish. When doors stay closed for too long, the mansion begins to feel different—colder, heavier, moldy, musty, and haunted by the past.

In the next chapter, we'll explore why the past doesn't stay in the past—and why avoiding those closed rooms only makes things worse.

# THREE
# THE HAUNTED HALLS OF MARRIAGE
## WHY THE PAST KEEPS COMING BACK

---

*The past is never where you think you left it.*
— Katherine Anne Porter

---

## THE MANSION BECOMES HAUNTED

I didn't realize it at first, but those closed rooms didn't just disappear.

- A door that isn't opened for too long starts to creak.
- A space that's left neglected for too long starts to gather dust.
- And if too many rooms are left abandoned, the entire mansion begins to feel haunted.

I walked through the halls of my marriage, and something felt... *off*.

I avoided certain conversations because I knew they would lead to conflict.

I noticed that my wife didn't seem as warm, as playful, as light-hearted.

There was a heaviness in the air, but I couldn't quite put my finger on why.

This is what happens when too many unresolved emotions go unacknowledged.

The mansion—the once-open, exciting place where love felt effortless—now had locked doors, unvisited rooms, and echoes of past pain that were never fully addressed.

And when my wife kept bringing up the past, she wasn't trying to punish me or dwell on negativity.

She was trying to open the doors, and freshen up what was inside the rooms.

## THE HIDDEN FORCES DRIVING THESE CONVERSATIONS

At the time, I didn't understand what was happening, but through my journey, I began to see that when our wives bring up something painful, three overlapping forces shape their emotions.

1. **Her insecurity** – Where she feels unloved, unsafe, or unseen.
2. **Her story** – What her thoughts are telling her caused this pain.
3. **Her strategy** – What she believes will fix the pain.

Where these three overlap, the emotional pressure builds—often landing squarely on us as husbands.

Oftentimes, as men, we focus on the precise, literal meaning of the words a woman uses to describe her *story* of how she came to feel as she does and her *strategy* for what would make it feel better. We react defensively, completely missing the real issue: *her pain.*

Take a look at this diagram I made to help my clients understand this:

## A "Svenn" Diagram: The Anatomy of Complaint and Criticism
*(Yes, some of my coaching clients actually call it that!)*

Their Insecurity
Where are they feeling
unloved or unsafe?

Blame
for You

Demands
for You

Their
Pain

Their Story
What Their Thoughts
Are Telling Them
Caused Their Pain

Dependency
on You

Their Strategy
What Their Thoughts
Are Telling Them
Fixes Their Pain

*Svenn Diagram: The Anatomy of Complaint and Criticism*

## WHY THIS FEELS LIKE BLAME (EVEN WHEN IT'S NOT)

AT THIS POINT, many of us might be thinking:

*"Okay, I get that she's bringing up the past because something feels unfinished for her. But if that's true, why does it always sound like she's blaming me? She really is blaming me! Are you trying to make me feel good about eating a shit sandwich?"*

That's a fair question.

Because let's be honest—when our wives bring up something from the past, it usually *doesn't* sound like an invitation to reconnect.

It sounds like:

- **Criticism:** *"You always do this."*
- **Accusation:** *"You never cared about how that made me feel."*
- **Demands:** *"I need you to understand this right now."*

And when we hear this, our natural response is to defend ourselves.

- *"I already apologized for that."*
- *"I don't even remember saying that!"*
- *"Why are we talking about this again?"*
- *"At what point will we stop having to revisit this?"*
- *"I'm sick and tired of your endless badgering. All you ever do is complain!"*

It really doesn't matter if she's blaming us when we are secure in the truth about who we are. With eight billion souls on this planet, there will always be people who misunderstand us.

How many of them need to see us correctly for us to be okay? Zero. Trying to control that is not a good use of our time, energy, and focus.

The only validation and approval we need is our own.

But here's the problem…

## BLAME ONLY FEELS LIKE AN ATTACK WHEN WE ARE INSECURE

This is going to be some hard truth.

When we don't fully trust in our own value, we depend on external validation to feel like we're enough. And when blame shows up, it *feels* like an attack on our worth.

What do we do when we think we're being attacked?

We defend.

But why defend something that isn't truly threatened?

Would we get defensive if our child blamed us unfairly?

Probably not—because we don't invest our self-worth in what a five-year-old thinks of us.

This is the real issue—not her blame, but our relationship with ourselves.

And here's the kicker...

The moment we stop defending, correcting, or dismissing, something unexpected happens:

The blame stops.

Now, I can't say with certainty if my wife actually stopped blaming me or if I simply stopped noticing it because I no longer saw it as a threat.

All I know is that **I no longer experience it as a problem.**

And that tells me something important:

**Her blame was noticeably proportional to my insecurity**

If blame bothers you, what you are feeling most is the pain of your insecurity.

Many guys get *really* mad at me for saying this. Yet, the ones who explore that discomfort more deeply tend to feel pretty powerful a year later, not because blame stops but because they addressed the deeper pain of their underlying insecurity.

## HOW OUR DEFENSIVENESS FEELS TO HER

When we defend ourselves, correct her, or try to move on too quickly, she doesn't hear logic.

She hears:

- *"Your feelings don't matter."*
- *"I don't care enough to understand."*
- *"You're on your own with this."*
- *"You're too much."*
- *"You're broken."*

And this is why so many men get locked in endless cycles of emotional misfires:[*]

1. She's trying to open a room.
2. We feel like we're being pulled into an argument.
3. She gets more upset when she feels us pulling away.
4. We shut down to avoid making things worse.
5. And round and round it goes.

So, how do we break the cycle?

## STOP MAKING YOUR REGARD FOR HER CONDITIONAL

I get it—this is hard to sort through.

She's trying to share something important.

But the message often comes inside a box that feels like it's filled with glass shards, razor blades, and hand grenades.

And because the delivery feels awful, many of us instinctively demand that she fix her packaging before we provide her with love, acceptance, strength, or presence.

In other words, we make our regard for her conditional.

And when we do this, we lose her trust.

For our wives, trust is everything.

To put this in perspective, imagine:

You get into bed with your wife, put your arm around her, and start initiating intimacy.

---

[*] This dynamic—where a man's defensive or withdrawn response to emotional tension gets **interpreted** as self-absorption—may also explain why so many women accuse their husbands of being **narcissists**.

A man who struggles to engage emotionally or meet his wife in her pain can come across as detached, indifferent, or even self-centered.

While true **narcissism** is a clinical disorder, many men get **unfairly labeled** simply because they lack the tools to navigate emotionally charged conversations with presence and empathy. They want to, but they're getting lost in the emotional intensity of their insecurity. Address this and she'll stop calling you a narcissist.

If this is something you've been accused of, I explore this in my book **Narcissist! Or Not?** with co-author Steve Horsmon from GoodGuys2GreatMen.

She pulls away and says, *"Nope. You didn't take the trash out like I asked you to."*

Or worse, *"You'll get no attention from me until you add an extra digit to your paycheck."*

Most of us would feel angry, hurt, or disrespected if our wife tied intimacy to a chore or a financial milestone.

And yet...

Many of us are doing this exact same thing emotionally—

withholding our warmth, our strength, and our love from our wife because we don't like the way she packages her emotional needs.

That's a transactional marriage, not a thriving one.

And if we want something different, we have to lead differently.

## HOW TO STOP FEELING LIKE WE'RE BEING BLAMED FOR EVERYTHING

At this point, we might be thinking:

*"So what are we supposed to do? Just take the blame for everything?"*

Nope.

This isn't about taking blame.

It's about taking *responsibility* for creating what we want.

It's about *leadership*.

And here's the key shift:

- Instead of getting defensive about her story, acknowledge her insecurity.
- Instead of resisting her strategy, listen for what she's really asking.
- Instead of shutting down, hold steady and stay present.
- Instead of focusing on the blame, see the pain behind it.

This doesn't mean agreeing with something that isn't true.

It doesn't mean rolling over or letting yourself be railroaded.

It means leading by being the grounded presence she's craving.

And it also means recognizing something that took me a long time to see:

### The "glass shards, razor blades, and hand grenades" aren't really hers. They're ours.

Yes, her words might be harsh. Yes, she might be blaming unfairly.

But let's be real—how many times have we expressed our own pain imperfectly?

Her words only cut deeply if they land on an open wound inside us.

When we're carrying insecurities—when we doubt our own worth, when we secretly fear we're not enough—her words don't just land.

They *explode*.

That's why we feel attacked. That's why we defend. That's why we shut down.

But here's the shift that changes everything:

Once we deal with our insecurities, those "glass shards" become nothing more than packing peanuts—annoying and clingy but ultimately *harmless*.

They don't cut anymore. They don't wound us. Most importantly, we stop living in the disempowering belief that other people must change before we can have internal peace. Instead, we take ownership and responsibility for that.

And when we're no longer *reacting* to pain that's coming from inside us, we stop making our presence and love conditional on how she delivers her pain.

- We stop demanding that she fix her packaging before we provide her with safety, warmth, and strength.
- We stop seeing her as the enemy and start seeing the real opportunity—to lead with love.
- We stop waiting for her to change before we step up as men.

This is how we grow in leadership.

It's not about *being right*. It's about *being resilient*.

It's about leading ourselves first—so that nothing she says can shake us from the man we choose to be.

And when we do?

Nine times out of ten, she fills that space with love.

This is *not* theory.

I've lived this myself.

I've helped men worldwide do it, too.

And brother, you can, too.


## THE TWO PATHS MEN TAKE WHEN FACING THIS CROSSROAD

At this point, we've got a **choice**.

When faced with this dynamic, men tend to take one of two paths.

One path keeps the cycle of distance, resentment, and frustration alive. The other leads to strength, confidence, and deeper connection.

And the difference between them?

How we respond.

Let me show you what this looks like in real life.

Here are two scenarios—two ways a man might respond when his wife brings up something painful from the past.

One leads to frustration, disconnection, and more of the same cycle.

The other leads to trust, healing, and an entirely new way of relating.

### Scenario 1: Defensiveness
### (What I Used to Do)

**Her:** *"I can't believe you didn't think to invite me when you went out with your friends. Do you even care how that makes me feel?"*

**Me:** *"What? I didn't think it was a big deal. I told you about it later. Why are you making this into a thing? Haven't we been over this?!"*

**Result:** She felt dismissed, unheard, and even more upset.

## Scenario 2: Emotional Leadership
## (What I Learned to Do Instead)

**Her:** *"I can't believe you didn't think to invite me when you went out with your friends. Do you even care how that makes me feel?"*

**Me:** *"I see that really hurt you. It sounds like you felt left out. That wasn't my intention, and I don't want you to feel that way. Say more about how that felt."*

**Result:** She felt heard. Her nervous system calmed down. The tension de-escalated.

See the difference? *(She can!)*

The second response didn't take the blame for something I didn't do—it simply acknowledged her emotional experience.

And when our wives feel emotionally understood, they stop pushing so hard to get their feelings across. In other words, the *story* and *strategy* aspects of their complaints grow dim.

- That's how we stop feeling like we're under attack.
- That's how we lead without losing ourselves.
- That's how we start unlocking doors instead of keeping them locked.

Which path will you choose?

## MAIN TAKEAWAY: IGNORING THE PAST DOESN'T ERASE IT—IT JUST CREATES DISTANCE

When our wives bring up the past, they're not trying to punish us.

They're trying to reconnect.

But if those moments feel like blame, it's because there's unresolved pain underneath.

Avoiding old wounds doesn't bring peace—it creates distance.

The only way to keep our mansion from becoming haunted is to learn how to step into those rooms without fear.

To do that, we must address our insecurities.

These moments of her "bring up the past" serve a vital purpose in bringing these insecurities to our awareness.

This is not a curse but a *gift*.

## NEXT UP: HOW'D THE ROOMS GET CLOSED?

Now that I've shared how I began to understand the haunted mansion, the next step is figuring out why the doors closed in the first place.

In the next chapter, we'll explore:

- The small moments that add up over time.
- How misunderstandings, unmet needs, and unspoken pain accumulate.
- Why men and women react to emotional closure differently.

By the end of the next chapter, we'll have a clearer picture of why our wives keep bringing up the past—and what we can do to start reopening those doors the right way.

# FOUR
# THE SILENT KILLERS OF CONNECTION
## HOW SMALL MOMENTS OF NEGLECT TURN INTO LOCKED DOORS

*Most people don't fall out of love. They stop doing the things that made them fall in love in the first place.*

— Unknown

### HOW A ONCE-OPEN MANSION BECOMES A PLACE OF UNSPOKEN TENSION

At the beginning of my marriage, the mansion felt alive, vibrant, and full of light.

Every room was open, and there was no hesitation in moving from one space to another.

We moved freely through it—sharing laughs, intimacy, deep conversations, and exciting new experiences.

But at some point, something changed.

It didn't happen all at once.

At first, it was subtle—a shift in the air.

- A door that used to open easily creaked when I tried to step inside.

- A once-welcoming space felt just a little colder.
- And over time, some doors stopped opening altogether.

At first, it didn't seem like a big deal.
*"It's fine. We'll just spend time in other rooms."*
But slowly, more rooms closed.
And one day, without even realizing how it happened, I woke up to find the mansion didn't feel the same anymore.

- I hesitated before bringing up certain topics, knowing they might lead to conflict.
- I avoided certain conversations because they felt like a trap.
- I sensed a growing distance, but I couldn't quite explain why.

This is how a mansion becomes haunted.
Not by a single catastrophic event but by a slow accumulation of moments—each one closing another door.
My marriage wasn't broken (yet–that would come later).
But it was changing.
And I didn't understand why.

## THE SUBTLE MOMENTS THAT CLOSE A ROOM

As men, we often assume that if something were a "big deal," we'd remember it.
But here's what I've learned:
Most rooms don't get shut by one dramatic, explosive event.
Most rooms get shut by a series of small, unnoticed moments.
It looks something like this:

### 1 . A wound happens.

It could be something small and unintentional, like dismissing her feelings during an argument.

It could be something more serious, like breaking a promise, shutting down emotionally, or saying something cutting in frustration.

### 2. She brings it up, hoping for understanding.

She isn't expecting me to fix it instantly—she just wants me to acknowledge it.

But if I respond with:

*"I don't want to talk about this again."*

*"I already apologized."*

*"Can't we just move forward?"*

*"That's it. I've reached my limit. I'm done. You're impossible."*

…then she feels alone in that room.

### 3. The room becomes uncomfortable.

At first, the door stays open, but there's tension inside.

Whenever that topic comes up, it feels uneasy.

She feels unheard. I feel criticized.

Neither of us wants to be in that room anymore.

### 4. Over time, the door shuts.

At first, it's just a little harder to enter.

But eventually, the room gets avoided completely.

She stops bringing up her feelings—not because they've disappeared, but because she doesn't believe it will help. She no longer trusts me with her heart. She's shielded, edgy, angry, and growing a bit resentful (*Side note: this can serve as a gift to allow her to see her own insecurities that must be addressed, but that's a subject for a whole other book!*)

I stop engaging—not because I don't care, but because I don't know how to fix it, and I'm tired of trying.

And just like that, another door closes.

## WHAT HAPPENS WHEN TOO MANY DOORS CLOSE?

A single closed door isn't the end of a marriage.

Every couple has moments of misalignment, misunderstanding, and repair.

But when too many doors close, the mansion becomes cold, distant, and filled with unspoken toxicity and tension.

### 1. The Mansion Feels Smaller

At the beginning of my marriage, my wife and I could go anywhere together.

Every conversation flowed freely. Every experience felt open-ended.

But as doors closed, there were fewer places we could go.

- Some conversations felt off-limits.
- Certain kinds of affection felt forced or absent.
- Emotional vulnerability felt like walking on eggshells.

Instead of moving through the mansion easily, we were confined to fewer and fewer spaces.

### 2. Emotional Distance Grows

When rooms close, so does emotional access to each other.

My wife, once open and expressive, became more guarded.

Once eager to connect, I became more hesitant and unsure.

We could still coexist in the same house, but the mansion wasn't alive with connection anymore.

We struggled to find mutual appreciation for one another.

We lost our joy.

### 3. Small Conflicts Feel Bigger

When doors are open, small disagreements stay small.

We have space to move past them. We trust that we'll find a resolution.

But when rooms are closed, every conflict feels more personal and more threatening.

- A simple disagreement over dinner turned into an argument about deeper resentments.
- A missed opportunity for connection became another sign that something was wrong.

When the mansion is haunted, every small problem echoes louder.

## THE PATTERN OF "TRYING TO MOVE ON" THAT MAKES IT WORSE

At a certain point, I recognized the growing distance.

And like countless men before me, I tried to move forward.

I thought:

*"We just need to stop focusing on the past and build new rooms. Onward!"*

And so I tried to:

- Plan date nights to "rekindle the spark."
- Focus on the future instead of talking about the past.
- Be more present in day-to-day interactions.
- Communicate more.
- Spend more time together.
- Have more sex.
- Learn each other's "love languages."

But because the closed rooms were never addressed, none of it fully worked.

No matter how many new rooms I tried to build, the past still lingered in the old ones.

My wife wasn't upset because she didn't appreciate my efforts.

She was upset because I was trying to move forward without first understanding what had been left behind.

## MAIN TAKEAWAY: HOW A ONCE-OPEN MANSION BECOMES A PLACE OF UNSPOKEN TENSION

The mansion of marriage doesn't become haunted overnight—it happens gradually, through small, unnoticed moments.

- When a wound isn't acknowledged, a door starts to close.
- When too many doors shut, emotional distance grows.
- The relationship starts to feel cold, distant, and full of unspoken tension.

The biggest mistake we, as men, make is thinking we can move forward without addressing the past.

We try to build new rooms without realizing that the past still lingers in the old ones.

But our wives aren't bringing up the past to punish us—they're bringing it up because they want to clear out the ghosts so they stop disrupting the present.

If we want to reopen the mansion, we must learn how to enter those rooms without fear.

Avoiding them only makes the tension worse.

Facing them with presence and confidence is the first step to restoring warmth, connection, and trust.

## NEXT UP: HOW JUDGMENT CLOSES MORE DOORS THAN YOU REALIZE

Now that we understand how rooms get shut, we need to go even deeper into why we, as men, resist entering them.

Because if you've ever wondered why your wife won't let things go…

Or why certain topics always resurface…

Or why some emotional conversations feel like a setup...

...then you're about to see why this happens—and how to change it.

Let's move forward.

# FIVE

# THE HIDDEN COST OF JUDGMENT
## HOW MISUNDERSTANDING SHUTS THE DOORS TO CONNECTION

---

*The greatest obstacle to discovery is not ignorance—it is the illusion of knowledge.*
— Daniel J. Boorstin

---

## HOW JUDGMENT ERODES CONNECTION

At this point, you might be wondering:
   *"Okay, but why does this even have to happen? Why do women hold onto things that should be over? Why can't they just move forward?"*

That's a fair question. And the answer has everything to do with perception—ours and theirs.

Often, we don't just observe how our wife moves through the mansion—we judge it.

And our wives often do the same to us.

- We see the way women revisit the past, process emotions, and communicate feelings—and call it *excessive, irrational,* or *counterproductive.*

- Our partners see the way we avoid some kinds of conversations, try to focus on solutions, and move on quickly—and call *cold*, *dismissive*, or *selfish*.

Neither is necessarily true. But when we believe our judgments are "the truth", we start reacting to our partner through the filter of those conclusions.

And, in my experience and observations, this a big part of how most marriages I encounter have slowly broken down.

## WE JUDGE WHAT WE DON'T UNDERSTAND

Think about how we describe the weather.

We say things like:

- When it's sunny outside, we say things like:
  - *"The weather is good today."*
  - *"It's a beautiful day."*
  - *"What wonderful weather."*
  - *"It's gorgeous out!"*
- When it's stormy, cold, or inconvenient, we say things like:
  - *"The weather sucks today."*
  - *"It's awful out."*
  - *"It's dreary and terribly cold."*

But the *reality* is, weather isn't any of those things—it's just weather. The words we are using to describe the weather are describing *our judgment of our experience* of the weather. Can you see that?

- A thunderstorm isn't *bad*—it serves a purpose.
- Rain doesn't *suck*.
- Cold isn't *terrible*
- A tornado isn't *evil*—it follows natural forces.

We attach meaning to weather based on how we experience it, not how it truly is.

And we do the same thing in relationships, and specifically, to the moods, emotions, and behaviors of our partner.

- We see women's wide emotional range, and we label it as *irrational* or *exhausting*.
- Women see men's emotional restraint, and they label it as *cold* or *disconnected*.

What if neither of us is wrong?

What if these are simply different ways of processing the world?

When we judge parts of our partner's experience as good and others as bad, we subtly signal that some natural, authentic parts of her are unacceptable to us. This breeds insecurity, pain—and more complaints.

To be blunt, behind every complaining woman is a woman feeling unloved. If her complaints are chronic, it's not proof that she's broken—it's proof that she has an unskilled lover.

When we grow as lovers, her complaints often fade.

Yeah... we know. Ouch.

I felt the sting of those words once, too. But I let them sink in, took them to heart, and now? I have a partner who is truly enjoyable to be around.

## THE STUBBORN PROBLEM: WE EXPECT EACH OTHER TO THINK & FEEL THE SAME

Here's where some of our biggest misunderstanding happens:

Most of us, at least starting out, treat women like they're just men with boobs.

We assume they think, feel, and process emotions the way we do —and get frustrated when they don't, concluding we've got a broken one.

And most women?

They treat us like we're just hairy, misbehaving women.

They assume we should engage in relationships and emotions the way they do—and can begin to think they've got a defective man when we don't.

And this is where so much marital conflict begins, because we can't build a great, connected, joyful and intimate connection on the mutual belief that one another is defective and broken.

Just about every man that coaches with me will eventually tell me what I call his "story about dysfunction" (SAD). That his explanation for how his wife got to be as dysfunctional as she is. Often, in the same session, he'll share his grief over the lack of connection they have.

He doesn't realize that he's living in a story that, to her, sounds something like this:

> *"Honey! You're one big hot chaotic mess,*
> *displeasing and broken in so many ways.*
>
> *When will you touch my wee wee again?"*

And I don't coach a lot of women, but they tell me their SAD story too, and do the same things in their own right, and to him, it sounds like this:

> *"Honey! You're one big disappointment of a male.*
> *A boy child who doesn't get it and.*
> *'m not very attracted to you or sure there's hope for you.*
>
> *Why don't you ever want to hold space for me?"*

Here's the thing: Instead of understanding, and embracing the natural differences between us, we judge the bejeezus out of one another, and then we try—often unconsciously—to reshape each other to fit our own expectations.

But here's the problem: those expectations are often contra-dictory.

## THE CONTRADICTIONS THAT PULL US APART

A part of us wants our wife to be more predictable, rational, and less emotionally chaotic. We want easy.

We thrive on structure, logic, and problem-solving, but her emotions don't operate like a lawn mower engine or a golf swing. Relationships don't follow neat, linear formulas.

We feel at ease when things make sense, when problems have clear solutions, and when emotions can be "fixed" like any other issue we tackle. But emotions—especially hers—don't work that way. The more we try to systematize, control, or suppress them, the more unpredictable and chaotic they seem to become.

At the same time, a part of every woman wants her husband to be more emotionally expressive, more attuned to her inner world—but without losing his steadiness.

She wants to feel our depth and vulnerability, but not in a way that makes her feel like she has to hold us up. She craves emotional connection, but also wants to be able to lean on us when she needs strength.

She wants us to just *know* what she's feeling without her having to explain it. To anticipate her needs without being told. To respond with the perfect mix of presence, intuition, and understanding—without her having to spell it out.

In other words, she wants something that isn't entirely in our nature.

And for us, there's a parallel contradiction. We want her to be more direct, logical, and steady—without losing the warmth, depth, and emotional vibrancy that make her who she is.

We are wired differently. But that difference isn't a flaw—it's an opportunity. If we try to reshape her into something more like us, we kill the very thing that drew us to her in the first place. If she tries to reshape us into something more like her, she loses the solid, grounded presence she actually craves.

The challenge isn't in changing *her* or in changing *ourselves* to meet impossible expectations. It's in learning how to navigate these differences in a way that strengthens both of us.

A part of every man does want his wife to be more logical, direct, and predictable in her communication—but without losing the softness, playfulness, and warmth that drew him to her in the first place.

He admires her flow, her emotional vibrancy, her ability to bring life and color into their world—but sometimes, those same qualities feel overwhelming, unpredictable, and impossible to navigate.

He wants to understand her, to engage with her emotions, but he also wants to experience her in a way that feels inviting, not chaotic.

## THE POLARITY GAP: HOW WE LOSE WHAT FIRST ATTRACTED US

In this tug-of-war, both partners start changing in ways that make them less attracted to each other. They usually believe they "have to" make one another happy and be good partners, but they become resentful for doing so.

- A man trying to "make her happy" becomes softer, more accommodating, and more emotionally available—but in a way that feels unnatural and emasculating.
- A woman, exhausted from feeling like the only one emotionally invested, starts hardening, guarding herself, and "becoming more like him"—but in a way that leaves her feeling angular, edgy, shielded, resentful, and disconnected.

Ironically, the more we try to meet each other's surface expectations, the more we lose what made the relationship magnetic in the first place—polarity.

Because it wasn't sameness that created attraction.

It was *difference*.

## HOW JUDGMENT CLOSES DOORS IN THE MANSION

Every time we judge her emotional world as wrong, excessive, overreacting, or frustrating, we pull back.

- We become less open, less available, and more avoidant.
- She feels less understood, more unheard, and more distant.
- The next time she brings up an old wound, we're already pre-loaded with frustration.
- She senses our withdrawal, so she pushes harder to be heard.

And just like that, another room in the mansion closes.

At first, these judgments might seem small.

But over time, they stack up, creating an entire blueprint of resentment, misunderstanding, and avoidance.

They become like a bank ledger filled with enormous amounts of emotional debits and very few emotional credits.

Pretty soon, you reach emotional bankruptcy.

## THE FIRST STEP TO REOPENING THE MANSION: LEADING BY GOING FIRST

Right now, we might be asking:

*"Okay, I get it. But what do I do about it?"*

That's exactly what we'll cover more in-depth in the next chapters.

But for now, the most important thing to recognize is this:

- Our wife isn't bringing up the past to punish us.
- She brings up the past because something still feels unfinished to her and her way of being; that seems like the best strategy.
- The key to rebuilding trust isn't avoiding the rooms—it's learning how to enter them without fear.
- And the very first step? Going first in acceptance.

Not approval. Not agreement. *Acceptance.*

Acceptance doesn't mean we endorse everything our wife says or does, that we're okay with every behavior, or that we stop judging her for who she is.

It means we stop assuming she should process emotions the way we do.

It means we stop labeling her as irrational, broken, or over-sensitive.

It means we stop telling ourselves stories about why she's not quite what we expected in a woman.

Leadership starts here. And by leadership, I don't mean control or dominance—I mean going first in the hard, unpleasant, uncomfortable, vulnerable work of acceptance.

## THE COMMON LEADERSHIP MISTAKE THAT KEEPS MEN STUCK

For a long time, I made the same mistake I now see in countless men.

I waited.

I waited for my wife to go first—to be more accepting, to stop judging, to chill out before I decided to let go of my own judgments.

I refused to budge until she did.

It sounded like this:

- *"I'm not gonna keep putting myself out there just to get shut down again."*
- *"Why should I keep trying when she's still upset about stuff from years ago?"*
- *"Every time I let my guard down, she finds something else to be upset about—what's the point?"*
- *"I'll start opening up when she stops making me feel like I'm always the problem."*
- *"I've already apologized. If that's not enough for her, I don't know what else to do."*
- *"Why should I keep showing up when all she does is focus on what I've done wrong?"*
- *"If she's not gonna appreciate what I am doing, I'm sure as hell not gonna keep trying."*
- *"I ain't doing nothing until she chills first."*
- *"She's the one making this hard. If she'd just drop it, things would be fine."*

- *"I'll stop judging her when she stops judging me!"*

A lot of men believe this is strength. I don't.

Strength isn't *reactive*.

Leadership isn't *abdication*.

When my values are dictated by how others act—rather than by my own clear and deliberate choices about who I want to be—I become powerless, emotionally unsafe, and untrustworthy.

Why?

Because I'm not leading myself—I'm being led by others.

## CAN THIS REALLY TURN THINGS AROUND?

It is common for couples' therapy and counseling models to emphasize working through issues together, side by side. In theory, that sounds fair—mutual effort, mutual progress. But in practice, the men I've worked with routinely report that leading this process—focusing on becoming a better *me* before trying to be a better *we*—without waiting for their wife to meet them halfway, has done more in a few weeks than years of therapy ever did."

Why?

Because when we fully lead ourselves out of judgment, we create something rare—an emotionally safe way of being within ourselves.

And that internal safety becomes the very thing our partner begins to trust.

Not instantly. Not overnight. Sometimes months later.

But eventually, when she no longer senses judgment—when she can feel that we're not measuring, comparing, dismissing, or bracing for battle—she begins to release her own judgments, too.

And in that moment, the gridlock begins to break.

Not because she changed first.

Not because we convinced her to think or act differently.

But because one of us had the courage to go first—to step out of the cycle of judgment and into something new.

That's how you get to a stage of marriage no longer steeped in mutual judgment and gridlock, but mutual acceptance.

## A TRUE PARTNERSHIP OF STRENGTHS

This is exactly where our natural drive to build, create, and move forward shines.

But we're not just patching up broken rooms—we're creating something new.

We're building a new way of relating to each other, one founded on mutual acceptance, warmth, kindness, understanding, and empathy. This relationship will be characterized by emotional safety and genuine connection.

And just like in any great partnership, we each bring something essential to the process:

- We build. She fills.
- We expand. She enriches.
- We create space. She brings life into it.

That's how it has always worked in the most deeply connected partnerships. Whether in homes, families, or relationships, when men create a strong foundation, women naturally bring warmth, beauty, and depth into it.

But here's the thing: before expansion can happen, we need to do some house cleaning and maintenance. That means working in the rooms we've tried to avoid.

## MAIN TAKEAWAY: JUDGMENT CREATES DISCONNECTION AND DISTANCE

The mansion of your marriage didn't become haunted overnight—it happened gradually, through small, unnoticed moments.

When a wound isn't acknowledged, a door starts to close.

When too many doors shut, emotional distance grows, and the relationship begins to feel cold, distant, and full of unspoken tension.

The biggest mistake men make is thinking they can move forward without addressing the past.

They try to build new rooms—more date nights, more affection, more presence—without realizing that the past still lingers in the old ones.

But your wife isn't bringing up the past to punish you—she's bringing it up because she wants to clear out the ghosts so they stop disrupting the present.

If you want to reopen the mansion, you must learn how to enter those rooms without fear.

Avoiding them only makes the tension worse.

Facing them with presence and confidence is the first step to restoring warmth, connection, and trust.

## NEXT UP: THE MARRIAGE TRAP: FIXING VS. UNDERSTANDING

By now, you understand why your wife's emotional world feels so different from yours.

But here's where a lot of men take a wrong turn:

They try to fix the mansion instead of understanding it.

And that single mistake—trying to solve emotional conversations like problems—is what makes so many relationships feel more exhausting than fulfilling.

In the next chapter, we'll explore:

- Why "fixing her feelings" always backfires
- How presence is more powerful than problem-solving
- The three simple shifts that make emotional conversations easier

Because the goal isn't to renovate the mansion.

It's to learn how to live in it—fully, openly, and without fear.

Let's move forward.

## SIX
# YOU CAN'T FIX YOUR WIFE'S FEELINGS—SO STOP TRYING
## WHY PROBLEM-SOLVING BACKFIRES AND WHAT TO DO INSTEAD

---

*When a woman is talking to you, listen to what she says with her eyes.*
— Victor Hugo

---

### SHE DOESN'T NEED A FIX—SHE NEEDS TO FEEL UNDERSTOOD

By now, we understand that men and women navigate the mansion differently. Hopefully, too, you see that a woman's emotions aren't problems to solve—they're invitations to connection.

Let's do a quick review:

- We, as men, move forward. We build, we solve, we assume that once something is settled, it's done.
- Women revisit rooms. They don't just seek closure—they need to feel that nothing unresolved is being carried forward.

This isn't a flaw in either of us. But when we judge it as one, we create distance.

And that's where many of us, as men, make a critical mistake. Instead of engaging with our wife's emotions, we try to fix them. And beneath that fixing instinct? Judgment.

Most of us don't even realize it, but we see emotions as problems:

- If something is messy, chaotic, or unpredictable, we assume it's broken.
- If something is upsetting, we assume it needs to be corrected.
- If something doesn't follow logic, we assume it doesn't make sense.

So when our wife brings up an unresolved hurt, we instinctively try to get rid of it—by solving, minimizing, or shutting down.

But here's the truth:

- Her emotions aren't broken.
- They don't need to be fixed.
- They don't need to be made "smaller" or more "logical" to be valid.

And if emotional conversations feel exhausting, it's not just because you don't know what to do—it's because you're judging the entire process as unnecessary.

## HOW OUR "FIXING INSTINCT" MAKES THINGS WORSE

Every man has been here:

Our wife is upset. She's bringing up something from before—something we thought was already settled.

Our instinct kicks in: *"Okay, how do I fix this?"*

So we try one of these:

- **The "Logical" Fix** – *"Look, I didn't mean it that way. I explained this before. Can we move forward?"*

- **The "Shut It Down" Fix** – *"Why are we talking about this again? We already solved this."*
- **The "Apologize and Move On" Fix** – *"I'm sorry, okay? Can we drop it now?"*
- **The "Overcompensate" Fix** – *"I'll just do better next time, I promise. I'll make it up to you. We'll go away next month - just you and me."*

And every time, it backfires.

- Instead of making her feel better, she gets more upset.
- Instead of de-escalating, the conversation intensifies.
- Instead of moving forward, it feels like you're stuck talking in circles.

And eventually, we throw up our hands in frustration, thinking: *"Nothing I do is ever good enough. She just wants to be upset."*
But that's not what's happening.
She doesn't want to stay in this conversation. She doesn't want to be upset.
She wants to feel *understood*.
And no amount of logic, dismissing, or apologizing will fix a lack of understanding.

## WHY PROBLEM-SOLVING FAILS IN EMOTIONAL CONVERSATIONS

We, as men, are wired to solve problems. I've spent my entire career as a professional problem solver. I'm good at it, and I enjoy it.
I bet you might too.

- When something is broken, we fix it.
- When something is inefficient, we optimize it.
- When something is in the past, we move on.

But a woman's emotions don't work like that.
Your wife's emotional pain isn't a *problem* to be solved.

It's an experience that needs to be felt, expressed, and processed.

**Imagine this:**

You and your gal are walking down a road, and she stubs her toe hard on a rock.

She's in pain and starts tearing up a little, trying to hold them back. She's holding her foot, saying, "That really hurt!"

Now, if you default to problem-solving, you might say:

*"Well, next time, just watch where you step."*

*"It's just a stubbed toe; it'll be fine."*

*"We're almost there—let's keep walking."*

But at that moment, she's not looking for a solution to prevent all future toe injuries, or your dedication to arriving at the destination.

She just wants acknowledgment, understanding, and presence:

*"Wow, that really hurt, huh?"*

*"Damn, that sucks—I hate when that happens."*

*"Are you okay? Let's sit down for a few minutes and take a look."*

That's it.

No fixing. No minimizing. Just presence.

And this is exactly how emotional conversations work.

She's not asking you to analyze, fix, or dismiss what she's feeling.

She's asking for *presence.*

And when we get this, everything changes.

## THE THREE SHIFTS THAT MAKE EMOTIONAL CONVERSATIONS EASY

So, how do we shift from fixing to understanding?

Here are three simple but powerful shifts:

**1. Shift from "How do I end this conversation?" →
"How can I make this woman feel seen and loved
and this moment feel safe?"**

Instead of focusing on getting past the conversation, focus on making the moment safe for her.

Try:

- *"Tell me more about what's coming up for you."*
- *"That makes sense. I can see why you'd feel that way."*

## 2. Shift from "Explaining why she shouldn't feel that way" → "Validating that it makes sense that she does."

You don't need to agree with everything she says.
You just need to validate that her experience makes sense.
Instead of:

- *"That's not what I meant."*
- *"You're overreacting."*

Try:

- *"I can see why that hurt you."*
- *"I didn't realize it felt that way for you—thank you for telling me."*

## 3. Shift from "Solving" → "Staying Present"

Instead of:

- *"So what do you want me to do about it?"*
- *"Here's what to do..."*
- *"If I were you, I'd..."*
- *"I don't know how to help you."*

Try:

- *"I'm here. I'm listening."*
- *"You're not alone in this."*
- *"How can I support you in this?"*

And here's the key:

She doesn't need you to become docile.

She doesn't need you to become more emotional than her.

She doesn't need you to become passive.

She needs you to be *steady*.

Grounded.

Unshaken by her emotions.

Not drowned in them.

That's what allows her to trust you.

## LEADING WITH AUTHENTICITY

This isn't about becoming more agreeable.

It's not about bending yourself into who you think she wants you to be.

It's about being fully yourself—grounded, steady, and unshaken.

Reconnection begins when we stop acting and performing and start leading from who we actually are.

That takes boldness.

That takes courage.

That takes self-acceptance and confidence.

Because without those, we don't show up as ourselves—we show up as a version of ourselves that we hope will win her approval. That's how a pesky need for validation leads us into the abyss.

And a man who is seeking approval isn't fully trustable.

The solution?

Go first.

Be more you—vulnerably, unapologetically, confidently—and invite her to do the same.

## WHEN YOU GET THIS, EVERYTHING GETS EASIER

Most of us, as men, assume emotional conversations are exhausting.

We brace for them like they're a root canal. We see them as long, drawn-out ordeals. We assume that if we engage, we're signing up for an endless loop of the same argument over and over.

But here's the truth:

- The more you fight against her emotions, the harder these conversations become.
- The more you try to fix or dismiss them, the longer they last.
- The more you shut down, the more they escalate.
- To a woman, that's like a lion being scared of a mouse.
- She also can't figure out why you're so afraid of something so inconsequential unless you think *she's* is something awful, too much, not enough, or that something is woefully wrong with her.

But when you stop fearfully resisting—when you stop trying to escape the moment—everything shifts.

Because when a woman feels fully understood, she naturally moves forward.

- No nagging.
- No repeating.
- No endless cycle of rehashing the same issue.

Just trust, connection, and deeper intimacy.

Once you understand this, the next step is to learn to confidently enter the rooms she invites you to.

That's what we'll explore next.

## MAIN TAKEAWAY: SHE DOESN'T NEED A FIX—SHE NEEDS TO FEEL UNDERSTOOD

Your instinct to solve problems and move forward isn't wrong—but when it comes to her emotions, it backfires.

If you want her to truly move forward, you have to stop fixing and start understanding.

Presence is more powerful than any solution.

Stop trying to make the conversation end.

Start making the moment feel safe.

That's what allows trust, connection, and intimacy to grow.

## NEXT UP: HOW TO ENTER A ROOM WITHOUT FEAR OR JUDGMENT

Understanding her emotions is the first step.

Now, we need to learn how to step into those conversations with confidence.

- Why men resist emotional conversations (and how to stop dreading them).
- The three keys to staying confident in hard conversations.
- How to move through any emotional "room" without losing yourself.

Because understanding is great—but you also need tools to stay strong, present, and engaged.

# PART TWO
# LEARNING TO WALK THE MANSION TOGETHER

## HOW TO LEAD WITHOUT GETTING LOST

# SEVEN
# WHY MEN DREAD EMOTIONAL CONVERSATIONS
## THE THREE FEARS THAT KEEP MEN STUCK

---

*Everything you want is on the other side of fear.*
— Jack Canfield

---

## WHY MEN RESIST ENTERING EMOTIONAL ROOMS

By now, we understand that avoiding emotional rooms doesn't make them disappear—it makes them haunted. The tension lingers, the unspoken hurts pile up, and the connection gradually erodes.

And we also understand that when our wife leads us back into these rooms, she isn't punishing us or clinging to the past—she's trying to clear out the unfinished business so it stops affecting the present.

Yet even knowing this, we still resist.

And that resistance isn't just about avoiding conflict—it's about fear and judgment.

Because let's be honest:

- Emotional conversations feel like traps.
- They bring us face-to-face with our own insecurities and shortcomings.
- The past feels like a black hole that keeps sucking us in.
- It feels easier to move on than to wade through emotions we don't fully understand.

At some point, every man has thought:

- *"I get that she needs me to be present, but what if I don't know what to say?"*
- *"What if she's so upset that nothing I do is good enough?"*
- *"What if I say the wrong thing and make it worse?"*

These are valid concerns.

And the truth is, most of us have been conditioned to avoid emotional spaces because we were never taught how to navigate them with confidence.

But here's the irony—women struggle with judgment, too.

Just like we might see emotions as chaotic and unnecessary, she might see our hesitation as cold, distant, or emotionally unavailable.

She assumes we're avoiding these conversations because we don't care—not realizing that we're uncertain how to engage without making things worse.

And this mutual misjudgment is what turns simple emotional differences into full-blown conflicts.

- We want her to be more predictable, logical, and rational— but we also love the warmth, intuition, and connection she brings into our lives.
- She wants us to be more emotionally expressive and attuned —but she also wants to lean on our steadiness and strength.

The problem isn't that we're different. The problem is that we assume the other should think, feel, and respond the way we do.

And that assumption—that her emotions shouldn't be happening, or that they should be "easier" to deal with—is why so many men resist stepping into these rooms.

But what if I told you there's a way to walk into any emotional room in your marriage—without fear, resentment, or losing yourself?

## THE THREE COMMON FEARS THAT KEEP MEN FROM ENTERING EMOTIONAL ROOMS

Before we talk about how to enter, let's talk about why we resist.

Because every man who struggles with emotional conversations is usually caught in one of three fears:

### Fear #1:
### "I'll Say the Wrong Thing and Make It Worse" →
### The Fear of *Uncertainty*

For many of us, not knowing what to say feels like failure. We like to have the right answer, to feel competent, to know that we're doing something well.

So when we're in a situation where there's no clear right answer, it triggers discomfort.

And our response? Avoidance.

- *"If I don't engage, I won't say the wrong thing."*
- *"If I don't step into this, I won't fail."*

But here's what actually happens:

- Avoidance doesn't make the problem go away—it makes it grow.
- Silence doesn't create safety—it creates more distance.
- And every time we avoid emotional conversations, we're training ourselves to distrust our ability to handle them.

The truth is that confidence doesn't come from knowing what to say—it comes from knowing that you don't need to have all the answers to stay present and engaged.

And when you show up anyway, you begin to prove to yourself that you're capable.

### Fear #2:
### "She'll Never Be Satisfied" →
### The Fear of *Emotional Exposure*

For many of us, this isn't just a fear of failing—it's a fear of exhaustion.

- We feel like we've tried before, but it never seemed to be enough.
- We feel like we've shown up, but the emotional tension still comes back.
- And we feel like if we open the door, it's never going to close.

So, we avoid.

But here's the real issue: This isn't about her—it's about us.

The real reason we avoid these rooms is because we don't trust our own emotional stamina.

We're afraid that if we engage fully, we'll end up feeling:

- Drained.
- Defeated.
- Powerless.

But the irony?

Engagement doesn't drain us—avoidance does.

When we step in, hold steady, and stay present, we don't just create emotional safety for her—we create it for ourselves.

We stop seeing emotions as a bottomless pit and start realizing that we can navigate them with confidence and control.

### Fear #3:
### "I'll Lose Myself" →
### The Fear of *Incompetence*

For most of us, stepping into emotional spaces isn't just about her emotions—it's about ours.

Because when she's upset, it doesn't just trigger a problem-solving instinct. It triggers something deeper:

Our own insecurities.

- If we feel accused, we might fear we're failing as a husband.
- If we feel blamed, we might fear we're not enough.
- If we feel powerless, we might fear we're not in control.

And when those feelings creep in, our instinct isn't to engage—it's to shut down.

But here's the truth:

Men don't struggle in emotional conversations because they're weak—they struggle because they don't trust themselves to stay strong inside them.

And that's the real opportunity here—not just to build emotional safety in your marriage, but to build self-trust inside yourself.

Every time you step into discomfort instead of avoiding it, you build:

- Emotional resilience.
- Unshakable confidence.
- The ability to lead yourself and others—without fear.

And that's why this process makes you stronger.

## HOW TO STEP INTO ANY EMOTIONAL ROOM WITH CONFIDENCE

Now that you know why you hesitate, let's talk about how to actually enter these conversations without fear.

Here's the three-step framework:

## 1. Stop Seeing Emotional Conversations as a Test
## —See Them as an Invitation

When your wife brings up a past hurt, some men react like a kid who just got handed a pop quiz in a class they hate.
They think:

- *"She's waiting for me to say the wrong thing."*
- *"She's trying to prove I'm not enough."*
- *"She's just looking for a fight."*

But what if she's actually saying:
*"This is a door I want to open with you because I want to be closer to you."*
The shift?
Instead of thinking, *"How do I survive this conversation?"*
Think, *"How do I use this as a chance to offer presence and connect?"*

## 2. Ground Yourself *Before* Entering the Room

Other men go into emotional conversations, already bracing for conflict or like they're about to get kicked in the groin.
They're already tense, already thinking of how to defend themselves.
But when you bring anxious, tense energy into the room, your wife picks up on it.
And she reacts to your energy before she even reacts to your words.
The solution?
Before engaging, take 30-90 seconds to ground yourself:

- Silently express gratitude for the opportunity to show up in your strength!

- Exhale slowly before speaking.
- Relax your shoulders and jaw.
- Remind yourself: "I am safe in this conversation."

When you bring calm confidence into a room, the entire conversation shifts.

### 3. Validate First, *then* Respond

The easiest way to step into an emotional conversation with confidence is to lead with validation.

Most men I meet make the mistake of trying to:

- Explain their side first.
- Justify why their wife shouldn't feel that way.
- Defend themselves from blame.

But before you explain, defend, or justify—start with validation.

- *"I can see why that upset you."*
- *"I hear you. That makes sense."*
- *"I get why this still feels like an open wound for you."*

Validation doesn't mean agreement.

It just means you're acknowledging *her* emotional reality.

And when a woman feels acknowledged, she softens.

She doesn't feel the need to keep proving why her feelings matter.

She doesn't feel alone in her experience.

And from that place, real conversations can happen.

## WHY THIS CHANGES EVERYTHING

When you learn to enter emotional rooms without fear, without defensiveness, and without fixing, everything shifts.

- Conversations become easier and shorter.
- Emotional cycles that used to repeat for years actually close.
- Your wife stops bringing up the past as often—because she finally feels heard.

And most importantly…

You become a man who is truly unshakable.

Because you're no longer afraid of emotions—yours or hers.

And that's when your marriage becomes a place of safety, not tension.

## FINAL CHALLENGE: CONFIDENCE GROWS BY SHOWING UP

If you take away one thing from this chapter, let it be this:

Confidence isn't something we earn by performance or perfection —it's something we discover, and uncover..

Many of us have spent our lives believing we have to achieve, perform, or prove something *before* we can trust ourselves.

But real confidence—the kind that makes us unshakable—doesn't come from outside of is (external validation) and it doesn't come *before* action.

It doesn't come from having all the right answers or knowing exactly what to do.

It comes from showing up, even when we feel uncertain.

It comes from leaning into discomfort and realizing that it doesn't break us.

It comes from stepping into the unknown and proving to ourselves that we were always more capable than we believed.

In other words, deep confidence comes *from* actions that take us into uncomfortable places where we discover we're enough.

And when we do that?

- The fear loses its grip.
- The judgment fades.

- And we realize that we never had to be perfect—just present.

This isn't about getting it right.

It's about becoming a man who trusts himself, no matter what room he steps into.

And that's what makes a man unshakable.

## MAIN TAKEAWAY: EMOTIONAL ROOMS AREN'T TRAPS—THEY'RE INVITATIONS

Many men resist emotional conversations because they fear saying the wrong thing, never being able to satisfy their wives, or losing themselves in the process. But avoiding emotional rooms doesn't protect you—it isolates you.

Your wife isn't pulling you into these conversations to test you or trap you. She's inviting you into a space where deeper trust, connection, and intimacy can be built.

This is what leadership in marriage looks like—not controlling her emotions, not avoiding them, but being strong enough to step into them without fear.

A man who can walk into any emotional room without running, fixing, or shutting down is a man his wife trusts deeply. And when she trusts you at that level, everything changes—

- The way she speaks to you.
- The way she responds to you.
- The way she desires you.

If you want to lead your marriage, start here.

## NEXT UP: CHAPTER 6 – WHAT YOUR WIFE REALLY WANTS WHEN SHE OPENS A ROOM

Now that you know how to enter emotional spaces confidently, the next step is to understand how to lead her through them.

Because when you know exactly what she needs in those moments—not just emotionally, but energetically—you become a man she trusts, respects, and feels drawn to in a way that goes beyond words.

Let's move forward.

# EIGHT

# SHE'S NOT SEARCHING FOR FLAWS—SHE'S ASKING IF SHE CAN TRUST YOU

## WHAT SHE REALLY WANTS WHEN SHE BRINGS UP THE PAST

---

*Trust is the fruit of a relationship in which you know you are loved.*
— Wm. Paul Young

---

## THE CONFUSION EVERY MAN FEELS IN EMOTIONAL CONVERSATIONS

By now, we understand that when our wife brings up something from the past, she's not trying to punish us—she's trying to reopen a room that still feels unresolved.

We also know that our job isn't to fix the room or escape it—it's to step into it with confidence and presence.

But even knowing this, there's still one huge question that baffles men:

**"What does she actually want from me when she brings this up?"**

We've all asked ourselves some version of this before:

- *"She keeps bringing up the same thing, but what am I supposed to do about it?"*
- *"If she doesn't want me to fix it, what does she want?"*
- *"How many times do we have to talk about this?"*

Married men often assume that if a woman brings up an old wound, she must be looking for one of three things:

1. **A solution** – But when we offer one, she gets even more upset.
2. **An apology** – But when we apologize, it doesn't seem to fix anything.
3. **A reason to stay angry** – But that just doesn't make sense.

So what does she actually want?

Here's where we get stuck. Deep down, we judge these conversations as unnecessary. We think, *If we've already talked about this, why are we still here?* That judgment—whether conscious or not—creates resistance before the conversation even begins. When we believe something shouldn't be happening, our instinct is to shut it down.

That's why emotional conversations feel like traps. Not because she's trying to punish us, but because we assume the conversation itself is the problem—when in reality, it's an opportunity.

That's what we're about to unpack in this chapter. Because once we understand what's happening beneath the surface, we'll never feel lost, trapped, or frustrated in emotional conversations again.

## THE REAL REASON SHE BRINGS IT UP AGAIN

Let's say our wife brings up something from two years ago—a moment when she felt unseen, unheard, or hurt.

We've already talked about it before.

Maybe we apologized. Maybe we explained our side. Maybe we both agreed to move on.

And yet, here it is again.

So we think:

*"If we already talked about this, why is it coming up again?"*

The answer is simple:

Because the emotional experience of that moment still exists in her body.

## THE OPEN LOOP THEORY OF EMOTIONAL PAIN

As men, we tend to process emotional experiences like completed events.

Once a conflict is "resolved" (*apology given, conversation had*), we assume it's settled.

Women, on the other hand, process emotional experiences like open loops—loops that only fully close when they feel:

- Heard
- Seen
- Validated
- Emotionally connected again

Psychologists have long observed that the brain holds onto unfinished experiences, treating them as "open loops" until they feel fully processed. Emotional pain follows the same pattern—until a painful moment is acknowledged, felt, and resolved, it lingers, resurfacing whenever something triggers it.

If a conversation ended but didn't give her full closure, then the emotional charge of that moment still exists in her.

And here's the part most of us don't realize—her emotions aren't the only thing keeping this loop open.

Our own emotional reaction plays a role, too. Because when she brings up something painful, it doesn't just remind her of what happened—it triggers our own feelings of failure, inadequacy, or frustration. And when we react from that place—either by shutting down, defending ourselves, or dismissing it—we keep the loop open instead of closing it.

It doesn't matter if it happened last month or five years ago—if the experience wasn't fully processed emotionally, it still lingers.

And the next time something even slightly reminds her of it, that emotional loop fires up again.

She's not revisiting this moment because she wants to rewrite history—she's revisiting it because she wants to feel different right now. If a moment from the past is still affecting her in the present, it's not 'over' for her. And that's what we're actually addressing—not the past itself, but the emotional experience that lingers today.

## WHY MEN NEED TO CLOSE THEIR OWN LOOPS, TOO

Right now, you might be thinking,

*"Okay, I get why she feels like she has unfinished business. But I don't. Why do I need to close this loop? Why can't we just move on?"*

Here's something I've come to believe after talking to hundreds of men every year, often in the midst of their darkest days: Men hold onto emotional loops just as much as women do–maybe even more so. We just don't recognize it.

We carry wounds from things that happened decades ago—times we felt unseen, disrespected, betrayed, or unappreciated. The difference? Most of us never consciously revisit those moments. Instead, we bury them. Then, our wife goes to bed without saying "good night," and we mope around for two days, feeling unappreciated and disrespected. That's not what she's being – that's an open loop from a really long time ago.

We're not as efficient as our wives with this. We distract ourselves with work.

We over-invest in achievements.

We withdraw from connection and intimacy.

We mope.

We numb ourselves with alcohol, porn, or overconsumption.

But the pain is still there—quietly shaping our reactions, our trust, our ability to connect.

And the mental health statistics for men? They paint a bleak picture. Men are lonelier, more depressed, and more prone to suicide than ever before. If we really didn't need to close emotional loops was truly a solution, wouldn't we be thriving?

So maybe—just maybe—we've been resisting the very thing that could actually help us heal.

## THE GIFT THE FEMININE OFFERS US

What if the way a woman instinctively revisits emotional wounds isn't just something to endure—but something that holds a gift for us, too?

What if her desire to "go back" is an invitation for us to finally face, feel, and release the things we've been carrying alone for years?

The masculine and feminine both have something profound to offer each other in the path to becoming our fullest selves.

- The masculine builds, moves forward, creates stability.
- The feminine processes, reflects, brings wholeness.

If we're willing to stop resisting and actually receive what she has to offer, we don't just help her feel safe. We become more whole men.

## CLOSING THE LOOPS FREES YOU BOTH

When a man learns to stay steady in emotional conversations, something powerful happens.

- His wife feels safer, which means she trusts more, softens more, and loves more.
- He feels lighter because instead of carrying the weight of his past alone, he finally lets it go.

This isn't about "giving in" to her emotions.

It's about becoming the kind of man who is free of his own ghosts.

And when a man is free? He leads differently. He stops reacting. He stops carrying the hidden resentment, the quiet loneliness, the low-grade disappointment that eats away at so many men's souls.

The irony? The thing some men resist the hardest—the emotional world of their partner—is often the very thing that could teach them a path to emotional freedom.

So, do we really want to keep dismissing this as "just how women are"?

Or is there something here we're meant to learn?

That's the real question.

## WHAT SHE'S ACTUALLY LOOKING FOR WHEN SHE OPENS A ROOM

Husbands assume that when a woman brings up an old emotional wound, she's looking for:

1. **A new explanation**–"*Maybe if I explain it better this time, she'll let it go.*"
2. **An apology to end the conversation**–"*Okay, I'm sorry. Can we drop it now?*"
3. **Proof that it wasn't a big deal**–"*You're overreacting. It wasn't like that.*"

None of these actually close the loop.

Because what she's really looking for is:

- A witness.
- A moment of attunement.
- An emotional connection that tells her she's not alone in what she felt.

The fastest way to help her move forward isn't to fix, defend, or escape.

It's to step into the room with her and acknowledge what happened—fully.

## HOW TO CLOSE AN EMOTIONAL LOOP (THE 3-STEP FORMULA)

So what do we actually do when she brings up something from the past?

Here's the three-step formula that actually works:

### Step 1: Acknowledge the Experience

Before we defend ourselves, explain our side, or try to fix it—just acknowledge what happened.

- *"I remember that."*
- *"Yeah, I can see why that moment hurt."*
- *"That was a rough night, I get it."*

This simple step immediately lowers her defenses because it tells her, *I'm not ignoring this.*

### Step 2: Validate Her Feelings

Validation is different from agreement.

We don't have to agree with her perspective to validate her emotional experience.

Try something like:

- *"I didn't fully understand how that moment felt for you back then, but I see it more now."*
- *"That must have been really frustrating for you."*
- *"I get why that memory still stings."*

Validation is what helps her release the emotional weight she's carrying.

### Step 3: Reconnect

It is common to try to end the conversation after an apology.
But what she really needs is to feel connected to us again.

- If the moment is light, a touch on her arm or a soft smile can shift the energy.

- If it's deeper, simply saying, *"I love you, and I want to keep getting better at this,"* can be powerful.

Once she feels emotionally safe again, the loop finally closes.

## WHY THIS FREES US FROM THE SAME OLD ARGUMENTS

We might be thinking, *"Why do I have to do all this? Shouldn't she just move on?"*

Here's the truth:

This isn't about giving in. It's about freeing ourselves.

Once she feels heard, the same old conversations stop coming up.

Once she feels seen, she no longer needs to prove her emotions matter.

And once she fully trusts that we're emotionally present with her, our relationship shifts into a place of real peace.

That's the goal.

## MAIN TAKEAWAY: SHE'S NOT LOOKING FOR A SOLUTION—SHE'S LOOKING FOR CONNECTION

When your wife brings up something from the past, it's not because she wants to stay stuck there—it's because the emotional experience still lingers for her. Men process emotions as events that end; women process emotions as open loops that need to be fully felt, acknowledged and closed.

The mistake some men make is trying to explain, defend, or fix the situation. But what she actually needs is:

- **A witness**—Someone to acknowledge what happened.
- **Validation**—A sign that her emotions make sense.
- **Reconnection**—A moment that reassures her she's not alone in this.

When a woman feels truly seen and understood, the emotional

loop naturally closes. She stops revisiting the past because she finally feels safe enough to move forward.

## NEXT UP: CHAPTER 7 - LEADING YOURSELF FIRST - STRENGTH & STABILITY IN THE MANSION

This is what leadership in marriage looks like—not controlling the past, not dismissing emotions, but being strong enough to step into them with presence. But if we want to lead our relationship with true confidence, we need something even deeper—the ability to stay unshakable, no matter what's happening emotionally in our marriage.

And that's exactly what we'll tackle in the next chapter.

Because the stronger we are, the easier this all becomes.

Let's move forward.

# NINE
# WE CAN'T LEAD HER IF WE'RE EMOTIONALLY FEEBLE
## HOW TO BEGIN BECOMING AN UNSHAKABLE MAN

---

*He who controls others may be powerful, but he who has mastered himself is mightier still.*

— Lao Tzu

---

## WHY EMOTIONAL STRENGTH IS THE KEY TO A THRIVING RELATIONSHIP

By now, we understand why our wife keeps bringing up the past and how to step into emotional rooms with confidence instead of fear. But before we can truly become the kind of man who moves through marriage with ease, stability, and deep connection, there's one final piece we need to master: emotional leadership.

Here's a reliable statement: we cannot lead our wife through the mansion if we are emotionally unsteady ourselves.

Many men approach emotional conversations already feeling anxious, defensive, or exhausted. I know I did. And it was because I was stepping into the room without first grounding myself.

- If emotional conversations feel exhausting, it's because we haven't yet built emotional endurance.
- If our wife's emotions feel overwhelming, it's because we haven't yet developed inner stability.
- If we lose ourselves in these conversations, it's because we haven't yet learned how to stand firm without collapsing or shutting down.

This chapter is about changing that. Once we learn to become emotionally solid within ourselves, we will not only handle these conversations better but also stop finding them difficult altogether.

## WHY SO MANY MEN FEEL EMOTIONALLY POWERLESS IN THEIR MARRIAGE

Let's be honest: a lot of us feel powerless in our relationship. We love our wife, we want things to work, and we're willing to put in the effort—but we feel like we're always playing defense.

It's like we're constantly reacting to the emotional climate, never setting the tone. We never feel like we're in control of the emotional tone of the relationship. And it's because of one key reason:

We are emotionally reactive instead of emotionally grounded.

I lived like this for years. I didn't even realize how much I was letting my wife's emotions dictate my own. I thought I was "just trying to keep the peace, " but I was really outsourcing my emotional stability to her mood.

## WHAT IT MEANS TO BE EMOTIONALLY REACTIVE

If we're emotionally reactive, our mood, confidence, and sense of well-being are entirely dependent on our wife's emotional state.

- If she's happy, we're happy.
- If she's upset, we're anxious.
- If she's distant, we start panicking.
- If she's affectionate, we relax.

This means our entire emotional state is at the mercy of whatever she's feeling at any given moment.

And when a man is in this reactive state, he is:

- Easily triggered in emotional conversations.
- Constantly trying to "manage" his wife's emotions instead of standing solid in his own.
- Prone to shutting down, withdrawing, or getting defensive instead of staying present.

And here's the part that changed everything for me: women can feel when a man is reactive (just ask em').

And it makes them feel emotionally unsafe.

Because if we collapse, panic, or lash out every time emotions are high, then she can't trust us to be the steady, grounded presence she needs.

## WHAT IT MEANS TO BE EMOTIONALLY GROUNDED & RESILIENT

A man who is emotionally grounded and resilient is steadily improving his internal leadership.

This means:

- He remains steady, no matter what emotional storm is happening around him.
- His confidence and well-being aren't dictated by his wife's mood.
- He doesn't need his wife to be "okay" in order for him to be okay.

And here's the paradox:

The more solid and emotionally steady a man is, the less reactive his wife becomes.

- When she feels our emotional strength, she relaxes.

- When she sees that we don't shut down, she trusts us more.
- When she feels our confidence in emotional spaces, her own emotions settle faster.

And the whole dynamic of the relationship changes.

This doesn't mean we are responsible for her emotional state. It means we stop being a contributor to the instability by reacting to it.

When we show up as a steady presence—not absorbing, not avoiding, not fixing, but simply being grounded and engaged—we create a space where emotional tension naturally diffuses.

It's not about controlling her emotions. It's about no longer being controlled by them.

And paradoxically, the more we embody this steadiness, the more she feels safe, connected, and able to move through her emotions without turbulence.

This is what true emotional leadership looks like.

Not force. Not control. Just the kind of presence that makes everything around it steadier.

## HOW TO BECOME AN EMOTIONALLY GROUNDED MAN (3 KEY SHIFTS)

### 1. Be the Lighthouse, Not the Rowboat.
### Shift from "Absorbing" Emotions →
### "Observing" Them

When their wives are upset, many men feel they have to absorb her emotions—taking on her stress, frustration, or sadness as if it were their own.

This leads to overwhelm, exhaustion, and feeling powerless.

The shift?

Stop absorbing. Start observing.

Imagine you're at sea during a storm.

Some men? They're the rowboat.

They get tossed around by the waves, pulled in every direction by their wife's emotions. The harder they row, the more exhausted they become—trying desperately to control the ocean instead of learning how to navigate it.

A grounded man? He's the lighthouse.

He stands steady. He observes the storm without being consumed by it.

- He doesn't jump into the crashing waves.
- He doesn't try to force the ocean to calm down.
- He doesn't let the storm define him.

Instead, he remains anchored, offering stability—a point of reference in the chaos.

His wife may be experiencing emotional turbulence, but she can look to him and know:

*He's not going anywhere. He's solid. He's safe.*

And when a woman feels that stability? The storm passes faster.

### 2. She's The River, Be The Riverbank.
### Shift from "Trying to Make Her Happy" →
### "Being a Steady Presence"

Many men believe their job is to make their wife happy—like trying to calm a river by smoothing out every ripple, clearing every obstruction, and controlling the flow. But the river is not meant to be controlled.

A man's role in marriage is not to manage the river—it's to be the riverbank.

A strong, clear, and steady riverbank provides structure, direction, and containment. It doesn't resist the river's movement; it channels it. But when a man is filled with the silt of insecurities, shame, and fear, his banks erode. The river spills over, flooding unpredictably. Other times, when he lacks self-awareness, clear values, or guiding principles, his banks become ambiguous—unable to shape the river's course.

The solution? Dredge the river and strengthen the banks.

- **Dredge the river** by clearing out the emotional debris—the shame, fears, anxieties, and insecurities that cause instability and reactivity.
- **Strengthen the banks** by defining your values, standards, and operating principles, so you can lead with clarity and steadiness.

The more solid, defined, and unwavering a man's presence is, the more freely and beautifully the river can flow. And paradoxically, the less he tries to manage the river, the more naturally it finds its course.

### 3. Stop Using Your Wife as Your Navigation System.
### Shift from "Reacting to Her Energy" →
### "Setting the Emotional Tone"

A man who lacks internal direction constantly looks to his wife to tell him where he stands:

- **If she's happy,** he assumes he's doing well.
- **If she's upset,** he assumes he's failing.
- **If she's distant,** he panics, thinking he's lost his way.

This is emotional reactivity—living as if she is the map, compass, and GPS all at once.

But a man who leads his life well doesn't rely on external instruments to tell him who he is.

He develops his own:

- **Compass** – A deep sense of direction that isn't thrown off by emotional storms.
- **Barometer** – The ability to read the emotional climate without assuming it defines him.
- **Thermometer** – The skill of gauging emotional intensity while remaining steady in himself.

- **GPS** – The wisdom to course-correct and adjust without losing sight of his destination.

The shift?

A reactive man panics at every shift. A resilient man stays the course.

A reactive man treats emotions like emergencies. A resilient man weathers them with steady leadership.

A reactive man follows her mood. A resilient man sets the tone

## WHY THESE SHIFTS MATTER

When we stop absorbing and start observing, we stop feeling like we're drowning in emotional waves.

When we stop reacting and start leading, we stop letting external conditions dictate who we are.

This isn't about ignoring your wife's emotions—it's about responding from a place of clarity, strength, and purpose.

That's leadership. That's resilience. That's what creates a marriage built on trust, respect, and deep connection.

## THE POWER OF EMOTIONAL LEADERSHIP

At the end of the day, our wife doesn't need us to be perfect.

She doesn't need us to never make mistakes.

She doesn't need us to always say the right thing.

But she does need us to be *steady* and *resilient*.

When we become the emotional leader of our own lives, every-thing changes.

- Our wife feels more emotionally safe with us.
- Emotional conversations stop feeling like battles.
- We feel strong, steady, and confident—no matter what happens.

## MAIN TAKEAWAY: EMOTIONAL STRENGTH IS THE FOUNDATION OF LEADERSHIP

If we're emotionally reactive, marriage will always feel like an exhausting game of defense.

But when we become emotionally grounded, everything changes.

- We stop absorbing emotions and start observing them.
- We stop trying to "make her happy" and start being a steady presence she can trust.
- We stop reacting to her energy and start leading the emotional tone of the relationship.

## NEXT UP: CHAPTER 8 – THE DAILY HABITS OF A HEALTHY MANSION

Now that you understand how to be emotionally solid in your relationship, the next chapter will show you how to keep the mansion thriving—without waiting for problems to show up.

Because the best relationships aren't built through big dramatic breakthroughs.

They're built through small, consistent actions that keep love, trust, and connection alive.

Let's move forward.

# PART THREE
# KEEPING THE MANSION OPEN & ALIVE

## BECAUSE WAITING UNTIL THERE'S A PROBLEM IS TOO LATE

# TEN

# MARRIAGE IS BUILT IN THE BORING MOMENTS
## WHY SMALL HABITS MATTER MORE THAN GRAND GESTURES

---

*Love is in the details.*
— Oprah Winfrey

---

## WHY WAITING FOR PROBLEMS TO SHOW UP IS A MISTAKE

As men, we often don't realize we need to nurture our marriage until something feels off. One day, we just notice it—our wife seems distant, arguments are happening more often, or intimacy has faded. Suddenly, we feel the urgency to do something about it.

- Our wife seems distant.
- Arguments are becoming more frequent.
- Intimacy has faded.
- Conversations feel more like logistical updates than real connections.

And when these signs show up, that's when they start trying. They suddenly want to:

- Communicate better.
- Be more affectionate.
- Spend more quality time together.

But by the time we realize things are off, our wife has often been feeling that disconnection for months—sometimes years.

The problem?

Some of us approach marriage like a car we poorly maintain—we don't think about it until the check engine light comes on or something breaks.

But healthy marriages (and cars) don't work well like that.

If we only pay attention to the mansion when something is breaking down, we'll always feel like we're playing catch up and defense.

Instead, the key is to proactively take care of the mansion—so it stays strong, connected, and fulfilling without constant repairs.

This chapter is about daily and weekly habits that keep your marriage thriving—without feeling forced, unnatural, or like another chore on your to-do list.

## WHY SMALL HABITS MATTER MORE THAN BIG GESTURES

Some of us also learned that keeping a marriage strong requires big, dramatic efforts.

- A fancy vacation to reconnect.
- A deep emotional talk to clear the air.
- A grand romantic gesture to bring back the spark.

But here's what I've discovered over the years:

Grand gestures might feel satisfying in the moment, but they don't sustain a relationship. What does? The small, daily habits that quietly build trust, warmth, and connection over time.

Why?

Because my big efforts can't override months (or years) of my neglect.

If we haven't been connected emotionally in six months, one "deep conversation" isn't going to fix it.

If we haven't been affectionate consistently, one big romantic gesture won't rekindle the spark.

Healthy relationships aren't built through occasional breakthroughs.

They're built through consistent patterns of connection.

And the good news?

We don't have to spend hours a day "working on our marriage."

We just need to build small, natural habits that keep the mansion open, connected, and strong.

## THE 5 ESSENTIAL DAILY HABITS OF A HEALTHY MARRIAGE

I'll be honest—I don't do these perfectly, nor do I try to!

Let me explain.

I'm not the kind of man who believes in brute-forcing relationship habits. I don't think the key to a great marriage is white-knuckling a list of routines and hoping they stick.

As an inside-out kind of man, husband, and coach, my approach is different and organic.

I believe the real goal isn't to "get better" at *doing* things—it's to get better at *being* the kind of man for whom these things happen naturally. The kind of man who lives in alignment with his deepest values, who moves through life with presence, openness, and generosity—not because he's checking off boxes, but because that's simply who he is.

My life as a homesteader has taught me that roots placed in good, healthy soil produce good fruit on the vine. The same is true here. These aren't just "habits" to force into your life—they're fruit that naturally accompany a man who is deeply rooted in emotional steadiness, integrity, and presence. If these don't come easily right now, it's not because you need to try harder. It's because the soil might need tending.

Some days, I'm better at this than others. Some days, I get distracted. Some days, I let life pull me out of that alignment. But I don't beat myself up over it, because I know that real strength, real leadership, isn't about executing routines flawlessly—it's about living in integrity with who I choose to be.

So as you read through these habits, don't see them as "homework" for your marriage. See them as indicators of deeper transformation—evidence of healthy roots. When you tend to the soil, the fruit takes care of itself.

## 1. Micro-Moments of Connection

I meet a lot of men who think connection requires big conversations or deep talks. I used to think this too. I meet a lot of men who make a dry heaving gesture when they learn this. Many women want no such things from their man. They want him to be the captain of keeping things light, easy, fun, and open, but trust he can lead to the deep places when necessary.

Research also shows that strong relationships aren't built on a few huge moments—they're built on thousands of small, daily micro-moments.[*]

I get frequently asked how much time Zelda and I spend together per day, and people are often surprised to find out it's not a grand amount - often 60-90 minutes or less of contiguous together time. Yet, we have tons of these daily micro-moments.

A micro-moment of connection is any tiny interaction that reinforces closeness, warmth, or affection.

Examples:

- A quick kiss before leaving the house (not just a rushed peck).

---

[*] Fredrickson, B. L. (2013). *Love 2.0: How Our Supreme Emotion Affects Everything We Feel, Think, Do, and Become.* New York: Hudson Street Press.

Research indicates that strong relationships are built on numerous small, daily interactions known as "micro-moments." Psychologist Barbara Fredrickson explains that these shared positive emotions, even brief ones, can significantly enhance happiness, health, and social connection.

For more, see: Fredrickson, B. L. (2013). *Love 2.0: How Our Supreme Emotion Affects Everything We Feel, Think, Do, and Become.* New York: Hudson Street Press.

- A genuine smile when she walks in the room.
- A touch on her lower back as you pass her in the kitchen.
- A playful tease, joke, or moment of light-heartedness.
- A hug, raspberries on the neck, and a dance dip.
- A playful smack on the bum as one another walks by.

These small moments take seconds but send a powerful message: *"We're still connected. I still see you. I value and treasure you."*

And when a relationship has hundreds of these micro-moments daily, emotional distance never has a chance to grow.

### 2. The "Six-Second Kiss" Standard

Most long-term couples eventually fall into habitual physical affection.

They might kiss each other hello or goodbye, but it's usually a quick, mechanical peck.

The problem?

Habitual affection doesn't generate emotional or sexual connection.

The solution?

A simple concept called the six-second kiss.

Every day, at least once, kiss your wife for at least six seconds.

- Not rushed.
- Not passive.
- Not just a quick peck.

Why six seconds? Meh...that part is irrelevant, and I just made it up for the book. Make it whatever you want. What really matters is that we slow down, savor the moment with our special person and that we shift our brains out of "autopilot," and actually focus on, and feel, the connection.

And when physical connection stays alive daily, it prevents slow-growing distance.

### 3. One Moment of Genuine Presence

In most relationships, couples talk all the time—but many, barely, if ever feel truly present with each other.

Many conversations happen:

- While multitasking.
- While distracted by work, kids, or phones.
- While mentally checked out.

But one moment of deep presence can be more powerful than hours of distracted conversation.

The habit?

Once a day, have a moment where you are fully, deeply present with her.

- Put your phone down.
- Make full eye contact.
- Turn your body toward her, squaring up face-to-face.
- Get close.
- Listen—not just to respond, but to truly hear.
- Let the moment last for as long as it naturally does.

Presence is the rarest form of attention in today's world.

And when a woman feels fully seen and heard, even for just a few moments a day, she feels emotionally safe and connected.

### 4. The "I Appreciate You" Habit

Over time, as a couple, we can easily stop verbally appreciating each other.

We assume, *"She knows I love her,"* and stop saying it.

But unspoken appreciation doesn't count.

A simple daily habit?

Once a day, I say one thing I appreciate about her.

It doesn't have to be deep—it just has to be specific.

- *"I appreciate how much effort you put into keeping our family organized."*
- *"I love how you always make our home feel warm and inviting."*
- *"You looked really good today."*
- *"I admired how passionate you were in your call with your sister and the way you encouraged her. You're a natural!"*

This takes less than 10 seconds.

But it counteracts resentment, builds goodwill, and reinforces connection.

### 5. The "End the Day Together" Habit

For some of us, bedtime is the only guaranteed time we're alone together.

Yet, instead of using it to connect, many us:

- Scroll our phones.
- Watch TV.
- Go to sleep at different times.

One of the simplest ways to keep the mansion open is to end the day with a moment of connection.

This could be:

- A short conversation before going to bed or falling asleep.
- A moment of physical closeness (even just lying together).
- A simple, intentional "goodnight" moment where we hold her for a few seconds.

These moments create emotional safety—reminding her that no matter what happened during the day, we're in this together.

## THE POWER OF THESE DAILY HABITS

Individually, these habits might seem small.
But when stacked together every day, they:

- Prevent emotional distance before it starts.
- Create a natural rhythm of connection.
- Build up enough goodwill that small conflicts don't turn into big ones.
- Make the relationship feel easy instead of effortful.

The best part? We don't have to carve out hours for this. These habits don't add more to our plate—they refine what we're already doing, making everyday moments richer and more intentional.

## WEEKLY & MONTHLY PRACTICES TO KEEP THE RELATIONSHIP STRONG

Beyond daily habits, a thriving relationship also benefits from a few weekly and monthly rituals.
These aren't huge commitments—but they create a consistent baseline of connection.

### 1. The Weekly "Us" Check-In

Once a week, take 5-10 minutes to check in with each other.

- *"How are you feeling about us this week?"*
- *"Is there anything we can improve?"*
- *"How are you feeling personally?"*

This keeps small issues from building up into resentment.

### 2. The Monthly Adventure Habit

Once a month, do something new together.

- A new restaurant.
- A short trip.
- A new activity.

New experiences refresh attraction and connection by breaking routine.

## WHAT IF THESE FEEL IMPOSSIBLE IN YOUR MARRIAGE?

I know that some of you reading this are married to a wife who feels emotionally distant, closed off, or even avoidant. Maybe you read through these habits and thought, *That sounds great, but my wife would never respond to this.*

If that's you, I want to acknowledge something upfront: You are not alone.

I've worked with many men in this exact position, and I know how painful it can feel. When your wife isn't warm, open, or responsive, these kinds of habits can seem pointless—like throwing effort into a void. And the instinct for many men is to try harder—to push more, initiate more, and seek more reassurance.

But here's the thing: these habits don't work as a means of *getting* something. They are for *giving*.

When a man starts doing these things with the unspoken expectation that his wife will respond a certain way, she can feel it–and it doesn't feel *good*. And when a woman—especially one with avoidant tendencies—feels even subtle pressure to connect, she instinctively pulls back even more.

For men in this situation, I recommend starting small and shifting focus inward.

Rather than trying to implement all of these habits at once, focus on #1, #4, and #5 micro habits and focus on open-handed invitations to the simple, fun, easy, and non-draining weekly and monthly practices.

- Micro-moments of connection—not to *get* a response, but to *give* presence.

- Expressing appreciation—not to *get* reciprocation, but to *give* regard.
- Ending the day with connection—even something as small as a warm goodnight, not to *get* assurance, but to *give* emotional safety.

And more importantly? Work on your own emotional steadiness, resilience, and fulfillment.

I've seen men transform these kinds of marriages—not by chasing, convincing, or working harder—but by becoming internally grounded, steady, and secure within themselves. And when that shift happens, something incredible follows: the dynamic begins to change.

This isn't something you have to figure out alone. If this resonates with you, I encourage you to seek mentoring or coaching (with someone like me) who has helped men in these dynamics. There's a way forward. You don't have to stay stuck.

The key takeaway? Don't white-knuckle these habits to force change in your wife. Use them as indicators of your own internal transformation. Because when you tend to the soil, the fruit takes care of itself.

## MAIN TAKEAWAY: SMALL DAILY HABITS KEEP THE MANSION OPEN

It's pretty common for me to not start working on their marriage until something feels wrong—but by then, disconnection has already taken root– and, boy, does this frustrate women!

- Big gestures don't save relationships—small, daily habits do.
- Micro-moments of connection prevent emotional distance before it starts.
- Consistency is more powerful than occasional effort.

A thriving marriage isn't built through grand romantic gestures or deep emotional conversations once in a while—it's built through daily moments of connection, appreciation, and presence. When you build these habits into your marriage, you don't just prevent problems—you create a relationship that feels effortless, fulfilling, and deeply connected every single day.

## NEXT UP: CHAPTER 9 - NAVIGATING THE HARDEST ROOMS (REAL-LIFE CHALLENGES)

Now that you know how to keep the mansion healthy daily, the next chapter will teach you how to handle the toughest rooms—betrayal, resentment, and long-standing wounds.

Because some rooms require deeper work to reopen.

And I'll show you exactly how to do it.

Let's move forward.

# ELEVEN

# SOME WOUNDS DON'T HEAL ON THEIR OWN

## HOW TO REBUILD TRUST, OVERCOME RESENTMENT, AND FACE THE HARDEST CONVERSATIONS

*Forgiveness does not change the past, but it does enlarge the future.*
— Paul Boese

## WHY SOME ROOMS FEEL IMPOSSIBLE TO REOPEN

By now, you understand how small wounds close rooms in the mansion of your marriage.

But what about the hardest rooms?

What about the rooms that have been locked for years—the ones filled with:

- Deep resentment.
- Betrayal (emotional or physical).
- Broken trust.
- Pain that was buried instead of healed.

Every marriage seems to have at least one room like this at some point.

And for many men, the hardest part isn't just stepping into these rooms—it's not knowing if it's even possible to open them again.

- *What if she'll never forgive me?*
- *What if the damage is too deep?*
- *What if I've already tried, and nothing has changed?*

The truth?

Even the hardest rooms can be reopened.

But not with the same approach that works for smaller wounds.

For these rooms, you need a different kind of presence, patience, and leadership.

This chapter is about showing you exactly how to do that.

## THE 3 TYPES OF HARD ROOMS IN MARRIAGE

Not all hard rooms are the same.

And to navigate them well, you need to understand the difference between them.

### 1. The Room of Unspoken Resentment

This is a room that neither of you openly talks about—but it's shaping the relationship in powerful ways.

- It's the sexual disconnection that's never been fully addressed.
- It's the years of feeling unappreciated that have built silent walls.
- It's the slow drift apart, where you feel like roommates instead of lovers.

You know something is off, but neither of you wants to be the first to bring it up.

Over time, these rooms create distance and numbness—not dramatic fights, but a quiet erosion of connection.

### 2. The Room of Broken Trust

This room is different.

It isn't just about neglect or disconnection—it's about a moment where trust was shattered.

- A betrayal (infidelity, lying, secrecy).
- A major failure to show up when she needed you most.
- A moment where she felt abandoned, unheard, or deeply wounded.

These rooms are the hardest to rebuild because trust, once broken, takes time to repair.

But it can be repaired—if you understand the right way to rebuild it.

### 3. The Room of Repeated Cycles

This is the room where the same argument happens over and over again—sometimes for years.

- The conversation about not feeling appreciated.
- The fight about emotional distance.
- The painful cycle of one person pursuing connection while the other withdraws.

These are rooms that never fully close—they stay slightly open, and every time you step inside, it feels like the same fight, the same feelings, the same exhaustion.

If you don't know how to break the cycle, it will keep repeating indefinitely.

## HOW TO REOPEN EACH ROOM (WITHOUT MAKING THINGS WORSE)

Each of these rooms requires a different approach.

Let's go step by step.

### 1. How to Reopen the Room of Unspoken Resentment

The hardest part of this room?

You have to be the one to open it first.

Your average fella waits for his wife to bring it up—but by the time she does, she's already full of frustration, exhaustion, or emotional detachment.

The key to reopening this room is to lead the conversation before resentment turns into disconnection.

How to Start the Conversation:

- *"I've been reflecting a lot on our relationship, and I want to understand if there are things I've been missing."*
- *"I don't want us to just be okay—I want us to thrive. And I want to know if there's anything I can do to bring us closer."*

The goal?

To invite her to open the room with you—without defensiveness or avoidance.

And when she does?

- Listen. Let her express what she's been feeling, even if it's hard to hear.
- Resist the urge to defend yourself. Just acknowledge, validate, and show her that her feelings are safe with you.
- Take small but consistent action. If she expresses a need, don't just promise change—demonstrate it daily.

This alone can break the cycle of growing resentment and create the space for reconnection.

### 2. How to Rebuild the Room of Broken Trust

When trust has been broken, many men either get defensive or overcompensate.

- They either say, *"It's in the past—why can't we move on?"*
- Or they go into fix-it mode, trying to prove their love with dramatic gestures.

Neither of these work.

The only way to repair broken trust is through consistent, quiet, reliable action over time.

3 Keys to Rebuilding Trust:

- **Transparency** – If trust is broken through secrecy (infidelity, lying, emotional betrayal), openness is the only antidote. No defensiveness. No hiding. Full honesty—even when it's uncomfortable. Broken trust can be healed.
- **Emotional Availability** – Trust isn't just about what we do —it's also about how present and connected we are. A woman can feel it if we're emotionally checked out. Show up fully.
- **Patience** – If we're the one who has broken the trust, she gets to heal at her own pace. The timeline isn't ours to control. It's up to us to show consistency, not urgency.

Most men I speak to about these things want to know how long it will take for her to trust them again.

The answer?

As long as it takes.

But the more steady and trustworthy you are, the shorter that timeline becomes.

### 3. How to Escape the Room of Repeated Cycles

If we keep having the same fight over and over again, it means:

- There's an underlying need that hasn't been met.
- The conversation keeps getting derailed into surface-level arguments.

The key?

Break the pattern by identifying the real issue underneath.

Next time an argument starts, pause and ask:

- *"What's the deeper thing you're feeling you really need from me right now?"*
- *"Are we having the same argument again? If so, what do we actually need to change?"*
- *"What would make you feel heard and understood right now?"*

By stepping away from the argument and into a conversation about the pattern, we can end the frustration cycle, reach a more effective resolution, and stop repeating the same fight.

## WHAT IF THE ROOM FEELS IMPOSSIBLE TO REOPEN?

Some rooms will feel so locked, painful, and haunted that we'll wonder if they can ever be healed.

If that's where you are, here's what to remember:

- No room is impossible to reopen—only rooms that require more time, patience, and trust to unlock.
- Our job isn't to force our partner into a room she's not ready to enter—it's to make it safe enough that she wants to step in with us.
- We can't control her willingness—but we can control how steady, present, and trustworthy we are.

Trying to force our way into a locked room never works. If anything, it makes her hold the door shut even tighter. But if we stand at the door with steadiness, openness, and no pressure—she may eventually open it on her own. And when she does, it won't be because we pushed—it'll be because she felt safe enough to try.

That being said, leading our marriages out of disconnection doesn't mean waiting forever. If we've been consistently showing up and leading with openness, and she's still completely unwilling to engage—then it's important to recognize that leadership isn't about waiting indefinitely. It's about standing strong in ourselves, keeping our hearts open, and knowing when we've done our part.

The goal isn't to force her through the door—it's to become the kind of man who creates an environment where connection can thrive. What she does with that is ultimately up to her.

## REINFORCING YOUR LEADERSHIP

Here's what I've seen, time and time again: We cannot lead our wives—or anyone—to a place we haven't yet gone within ourselves. And yet, so many of us have tried to open our wife's heart without first doing the work to open our own.

The problem? We cannot lead from a place of emotional disconnection.

If we haven't gone into the locked rooms inside ourselves...

If we haven't faced our own fears, wounds, and patterns...

If we haven't built our own inner security...

Then, trying to open her locked rooms will only create resistance.

Many of us, whether we realize it or not, have tried to "rescue" our wives from emotional distance—not because we were leading but because we wanted to feel like heroes.

We looked for validation in how much we could fix, how much we were needed, or how much she responded to us.

But this isn't leadership.

It's emotional *dependency*; it's toxic to relationships, most of all, the one with yourself.

And it's not entirely loving—often, it's manipulative, disingenuous, and self-serving.

The important takeaway is this: leadership isn't about getting changes to take place within other people. It's about becoming men who are so deeply rooted in our own self-worth, agency, and personal power that she feels safe enough and inspired to open up on her own.

## OPEN MEN INVITE OPEN WOMEN

The best place to focus our energy isn't on trying to "get her to open up."

It's on going deeper into *our* mansion—exploring every locked room, cleaning out old baggage, and stepping fully into our own wholeness.

Because when we do?

We naturally become the kind of men our wives want to open up to.

And that is leadership.

## MAIN TAKEAWAY: EVEN THE HARDEST ROOMS CAN BE REOPENED

Some rooms in your marriage feel locked forever—resentment, betrayal, and repeated conflicts that seem impossible to resolve. But even the most haunted rooms can be reopened if you approach them with patience, leadership, and the right mindset.

- Resentment fades when you lead the conversation instead of waiting for it to explode.
- Broken trust isn't fixed by words—it's rebuilt through quiet, consistent actions over time.
- Repeated conflicts don't change unless you address the real issue beneath the surface.

Healing doesn't happen by forcing a room open or demanding your wife "just move on." It happens when you create an environment safe enough for her to want to walk through that door with you.

Lead with steady presence, not urgency. Stay the course, and even the hardest rooms can become places of connection once again.

## NEXT UP: CHAPTER 10 – THE MANSION AS A PLACE OF LOVE, NOT WAR

This final chapter is about shifting the entire mindset of how you see marriage.

Because the goal isn't just to repair wounds—it's to build a marriage that is:

- Full of playfulness and deep connection.
- Built on trust, safety, and mutual appreciation.
- A place where love can grow—not just survive.

Let's move forward.

# TWELVE
# STOP PLAYING DEFENSE AND START LEADING

## HOW TO BUILD A MARRIAGE THAT'S STRONG, PASSIONATE, AND UNSHAKABLE

---

*A ship in harbor is safe, but that is not what ships are built for.*
— John A. Shedd

---

## WHY MOST MARRIAGES SLOWLY TURN INTO BATTLEGROUNDS

At the beginning of your relationship, your mansion was full of life, excitement, and connection.

There were no locked doors yet. No emotional landmines waiting to go off. No years of accumulated pain, frustration, or misunderstanding.

But over time, something shifted.

You started noticing:

- More arguments about the same things.
- More emotional distance, even when things were "fine."
- More times where you felt like you were on opposing teams instead of partners.

And at some point, without even realizing it, the mansion started feeling less like a home and more like a battleground.

Instead of feeling safe and inviting, some rooms started to feel tense, unpredictable, or outright hostile.

- Arguments became about who was "right" instead of what actually mattered.
- Silence became a shield, a way to avoid fights instead of facing them.
- Connection became something that only happened in rare, fleeting moments.

If you've ever felt like your marriage has become a cycle of conflict, withdrawal, or emotional exhaustion, you're not alone.

But here's the truth too many men never realize:

Your marriage will always be either a place of love or a place of war.

And the difference isn't about whether or not you fight—*it's about how you move through conflict and connection.*

This chapter is about making your mansion a place of love, warmth, and deep trust again—no matter how many battles have been fought inside it.

## HOW LOVE SLOWLY GETS REPLACED BY RESENTMENT

None of us wake up one day and decide, *"Let's make life harder for each other."*

But many of us have woken up years into marriage and realized that love doesn't feel like love anymore.

So how does it happen?

Here's how it happens to so many of us as men:

### Step 1: The Small Injuries Begin

- We break a promise—maybe something small.
- She distances herself, but we assume it's temporary.

- We brush it off, thinking everything is fine.

### Step 2: One of Us Feels Unseen or Unheard

- She brings up something that's been bothering her, and we dismiss it.
- We try to express a need, and she doesn't seem to respond.
- Neither of us means to hurt the other, but something shifts.

### Step 3: We Start Protecting Ourselves Instead of Each Other

- Instead of talking about it, we retreat or get defensive.
- Frustrations build up, but we don't bring them into the open.
- We start making assumptions about her intentions.

### Step 4: Every Conflict Starts to Feel Heavier

- A forgotten errand becomes proof that we're not appreciated.
- A disagreement turns into another "we're just too different" argument.
- We aren't just fighting about today—we're fighting through the lens of everything unsaid.

### Step 5: Love Feels Like a Struggle

- Affection fades because neither of us feels emotionally safe.
- Conversations feel more like obligations than moments of connection.
- The mansion stops feeling like home and starts feeling like a place to manage, not enjoy.

And this is how so many of us turn love into a battle—not through one big fight, but through years of small, unresolved ones.

## HOW TO TURN THE MANSION BACK INTO A PLACE OF LOVE

The good news?

Even if your mansion has been filled with battles, it can become a place of love again.

But it requires two key shifts in how you approach conflict, connection, and leadership.

## SHIFT #1: MOVE FROM "WINNING" TO UNDERSTANDING

Most couples, when they fight, aren't actually trying to solve problems.

They're trying to win.

- They want to prove their point.
- They want the other person to admit they were wrong.
- They want validation, not resolution.

And this is where a lot of men go wrong in emotional conversations.

They approach their wife's emotions like a debate to win instead of an experience to understand.

And as long as you're in debate mode, the mansion will always feel like a battleground instead of a place of love.

The solution?

Replace "winning" with curiosity.

Instead of thinking:

- *"She's wrong about this."*
- *"I need to prove my point."*
- *"She just doesn't get it."*

Shift to:

- *"What's really underneath what she's saying?"*
- *"What would help her feel truly heard right now?"*
- *"What would create closeness, not more distance?"*

Men who make this shift stop feeling like every conflict is a fight they need to endure.

Instead, they start seeing it as an opportunity to reconnect, even in disagreement.

## SHIFT #2: LEAD WITH LOVE, EVEN WHEN IT FEELS UNDESERVED

Many men hold the pole position of reactively in their marriage.

This means:

- If their wife is affectionate, they respond with affection.
- If she's distant, they become distant too.
- If she's upset, they either shut down or get defensive.

This is not leadership.

This is following.

A man who waits for his wife to set the emotional tone of the relationship isn't leading—he's reacting.

The shift?

Lead with love, regardless of her mood, energy, or emotions.

This doesn't mean being a doormat.

It means:

- Being affectionate, even when she's in a mood.
- Staying open and engaged, even when she's distant.
- Being consistent in how you show up—without waiting for her to be "deserving" of it.

And here's the paradox:

The more solid and loving you are, the more she naturally responds in kind.

Women don't want to lead the emotional tone of the relationship.

They want a man who is strong, steady, and open—even when things aren't perfect.

And the men who master this turn their marriage into a place of love—not war.

## FIRST, LEAD YOURSELF

Here's what I've seen in working with so many men: We cannot lead our wife into a thriving relationship if we haven't first led ourselves there.

So many of us have tried to lead our marriage into love, connection, and trust while our own inner mansion is full of locked doors.

We try to pull our wife into a place of deeper intimacy—without having first opened those places inside ourselves.

But it doesn't work.

Because, as I mentioned previously, open men open women.

If we haven't done the work to clean up our own self-judgment, shame, dependency, insecurity, and and emotional avoidance, how can we expect her to trust that the mansion is safe?

- If we are reactive, she will brace herself.
- If we are emotionally closed, she will keep her walls up.
- If we are waiting for her to lead, we are following, not leading.

And this is the mistake many of us make—we try to lead by changing her, instead of first becoming the man she naturally wants to open up to.

The key isn't in convincing her to come closer—it's in becoming a man who creates emotional safety, trust, and depth simply by how we show up.

If we do this, the mansion stops feeling like a battleground.

It starts to feel like home again.

## WHAT A LOVE-FILLED MANSION FEELS LIKE

When a marriage is truly healthy, thriving, and full of love, here's what happens:

- Fights become shorter, less frequent, and more productive.
- Your wife stops bringing up the past as often—because she feels truly heard.
- Sexual connection becomes easy, natural, and mutual.
- Conversations feel warm, not cold or transactional.
- Your home feels like a place of peace, not tension.

This is what happens when the mansion is truly open again.

## BRINGING IT ALL TOGETHER

If you've read this far, it means you're not just looking for quick fixes or short-term hacks.

You want real change.

And here's the truth:

The difference between men who stay stuck in cycles of conflict, frustration, and resentment and the men who build thriving, connected, powerful marriages is simple:

- They stop waiting for their wife to lead the relationship.
- They take ownership of how they show up.
- They become men who can step into any emotional space with confidence, strength, and presence.

And when you become that man, the mansion of your marriage doesn't just stay open.

It becomes a place of love, warmth, trust, and passion—for life.

## YOUR NEXT STEPS

If you've read this far, it means you aren't just looking for quick fixes.

You want real change.

And here's the truth we have to face as men:

No one is coming to lead our marriage for us.

If we want a relationship built on trust, love, and deep connection, we have to be the men who lead it there.

That means:

- We stop waiting for her to go first.
- We stop measuring whether she "deserves" our love.
- We lead, even when it's hard.

Because a thriving relationship doesn't happen by accident.

It happens when a man steps fully into his own self-leadership, removes his own judgments, and creates a marriage where love, trust, and connection naturally thrive.

The mansion is waiting.

The doors are ready to open.

But you have to be the one to take the first step.

Are you ready?

# PART FOUR
# STRATEGIES FOR SUCCESS & FAILURE

A PRACTICAL GUIDE TO STOP MAKING THINGS WORSE AND START LEADING WITH CONFIDENCE.

# THIRTEEN
# THE "YEAH, BUT..." OBJECTIONS THAT KEEP MEN STUCK

## AND HOW TO CRUSH THEM

---

*The chains of habit are too weak to be felt until they are too strong to be broken.*

— Samuel Johnson

---

## WHY IT'S NORMAL TO RESIST CHANGE (AND WHY THAT'S NOT THE PROBLEM)

I f you've been reading this book and catching yourself thinking, *Yeah, but...*—you're not alone. In fact, that's a good thing.

Skepticism is a sign of intelligence. Resistance is a sign that your mind is actively engaged, questioning, and filtering new ideas through your existing beliefs and experiences. That's what thinking men do. We don't just blindly accept everything we hear—we measure it, weigh it, and challenge it.

And that's exactly what you *should* do.

If you didn't have any "Yeah, but..." moments while reading this book, I'd be worried. Because that would mean you weren't actually engaging with the material—you'd just be nodding along, treating it like motivational fluff, instead of seriously considering how it applies to your life.

The real problem isn't having objections—it's getting stuck in them.

A *healthy* "Yeah, but…" is an invitation to deeper understanding. It's a moment of critical thinking where you're testing a new idea against what you already know. But an *unhealthy* "Yeah, but…" is a shield—an excuse to avoid discomfort, a justification to stay the same, a way to shift responsibility away from yourself.

I know this because I've lived it. I spent years pushing back on advice that challenged me, convinced that my situation was different, that my wife was the real problem, that I had already tried everything and nothing worked. But looking back, I can see that most of my objections weren't based in truth—they were based in fear.

Fear that I'd have to change more than I wanted to.

Fear that even if I did change, nothing would get better.

Fear that I'd put in the work and still be rejected.

The key to moving forward isn't pretending those fears don't exist. It's acknowledging them and deciding to lead anyway.

So in this chapter, we're going to address the most common "Yeah, but…" objections that keep men stuck. Not to dismiss them, but to unpack them—to see whether they're valid concerns or just old patterns keeping you trapped.

Because at the end of the day, your objections aren't the problem. It's what you *do* with them that determines whether you stay stuck or step forward.

## "YEAH, BUT MY WIFE JUST WON'T LET THINGS GO. NOTHING I DO IS EVER ENOUGH."

I get it. I really do. I used to feel the same way—like I was constantly on trial for past mistakes, no matter how much I tried to prove myself. It felt like my wife had an infinite memory for my failures, but a short-term one for anything good I did.

Here's what I eventually realized: She wasn't bringing up the past to punish me—she was bringing it up because she didn't feel fully safe yet.

Women don't hold onto pain because they enjoy it. They hold onto it because something inside them hasn't found closure. If she keeps circling back, it's because the emotional wound never fully healed.

You might be thinking, *"But I already apologized! What else am I supposed to do?"*

Apologizing is great. But an apology without a deeper emotional shift is like slapping a bandage on a wound without treating the infection. She doesn't just want a "sorry"—she wants to feel that you truly understand her pain, that you take ownership, and that she's safe from it happening again.

That's when things changed for me. Instead of getting frustrated that she "wouldn't let it go," I started leaning in—listening more, reacting less, and actually leading us out of the cycle instead of just defending myself. And when she saw that shift, she stopped bringing up the past.

**What to Do:** Next time she brings up an old hurt, instead of saying, *"Why are we talking about this again?"* try, *"I see this still really hurts you. I don't want you carrying that pain. Tell me more about what you need to feel safe with me again."*

## "YEAH, BUT SHE'S THE ONE WHO KEEPS STARTING FIGHTS, NOT ME."

I used to tell myself this all the time. *"She's the one who keeps bringing up problems. If she just stopped, we'd be fine."*

What I didn't see was that her "starting fights" wasn't about wanting conflict—it was about wanting connection.

For many women, conflict is the doorway to intimacy. If something feels unresolved, she can't ignore it and move on like you might. She needs to work through it emotionally before she can fully let it go.

That's why avoiding conflict doesn't bring peace—it just delays the explosion. When I finally stopped seeing her emotional outbursts as "attacks" and started seeing them as calls for connection, our whole dynamic shifted.

**What to Do:** Instead of shutting her down, try responding with, *"It sounds like something's really bothering you. Let's talk—I want to understand."* That one shift alone can transform your marriage.


## "YEAH, BUT I ALREADY APOLOGIZED. HOW MANY TIMES DO I HAVE TO DO IT?"

I used to think apologies were transactions—you say "I'm sorry," she forgives, and you both move on. But true healing isn't transactional —it's relational.

When you break trust, your wife doesn't just need a one-time "I'm sorry"—she needs repeated proof that you're safe, trustworthy, and emotionally present.

Think about it like this: If someone wrecked your car, would one "sorry" be enough? Or would you need time, reassurance, and actions that prove they're a different driver now?

That's what your wife is looking for. Consistency. Presence. A sense that the past is actually staying in the past—not because she "let it go," but because you've truly changed.

**What to Do:** Instead of being frustrated that she "still doesn't trust me," ask yourself, *"How can I SHOW her that I'm the man she can fully trust?"*


## "YEAH, BUT SHE SHOULD BE THE ONE WORKING ON THIS TOO. WHY IS IT ALL ON ME?"

This one stung when I first had to face it. I wanted to believe that marriage was 50/50—that if I was going to put in effort, she should too.

But here's the brutal truth: You can't lead your marriage by waiting for her to meet you halfway.

The minute you say, *"I'll step up when she does,"* you've already lost leadership.

I had to learn that my job wasn't to wait for her to change—it was to lead the change I wanted to see. And when I did? She naturally followed.

**What to Do:** Instead of waiting for her to match your effort, ask, *"What kind of man do I need to be to create the marriage I want?"*

## "YEAH, BUT IF I STOP DEFENDING MYSELF, WON'T I JUST BE LETTING HER WALK ALL OVER ME?"

I used to think standing my ground made me strong—but all it really did was make me defensive, disconnected, and stuck in power struggles.

Real strength isn't about proving you're right—it's about holding your frame, staying calm, and being emotionally unshakable even when she's upset.

**What to Do:** Next time she's upset, instead of jumping to defend yourself, try this: *"I see how important this is to you. Let's talk about it."*

## "YEAH, BUT SHE'S THE ONE WHO HURT ME FIRST. WHY SHOULD I BE THE ONE TO FIX THINGS?"

I used to hold onto this one like a shield, justifying my inaction because, after all, *wasn't she the one who did something wrong first?*

Maybe your wife betrayed your trust, dismissed your feelings, or failed to meet you where you needed her most. Maybe she cut deep in ways that still ache.

So, let me be clear: You're not wrong to feel hurt.

But here's the brutal truth—waiting for her to fix what she broke won't heal you.

I learned this the hard way. I spent years quietly resenting my wife for the ways I felt hurt or unappreciated, thinking, *"If she really cared, she'd be the one trying harder."* But that mindset only kept us stuck.

It wasn't until I stopped focusing on who started it and started focusing on who would lead out of it that real change happened.

Does that mean ignoring what she did? No. It means owning how you respond to it. It means deciding whether you want to stay locked in resentment or lead your marriage back to something worth fighting for.

**What to Do:** Ask yourself, *"Do I want to be right, or do I want to be free?"* Resentment might feel justified, but leadership means choosing to lead, even when you weren't the one who caused the damage.

## "YEAH, BUT SHE NEVER APPRECIATES THE THINGS I ACTUALLY DO RIGHT."

Man, this one used to eat me up. I worked my ass off to provide, to be a good husband, to show up—and it felt like she never saw it.

At one point, I even told myself, *"If she's not going to appreciate me, why should I even bother?"*

But here's what I eventually had to face: I was keeping score in a way that wasn't helping either of us.

I wanted her to appreciate the things I did, but I wasn't paying attention to what she actually needed from me.

See, men and women often express love differently. You might be showing love in ways that make sense to you, but if they don't land with her, she won't feel it.

It wasn't until I stopped focusing on what I wasn't getting and started focusing on how to better connect with her needs that I saw a shift. And when she felt more emotionally safe and connected to me, the appreciation followed naturally.

**What to Do:** Instead of thinking, *"She never appreciates what I do,"* ask, *"Does she feel loved in a way that actually lands for her?"* Leading means giving without keeping score.

## "YEAH, BUT I'M JUST NOT A NATURALLY EMOTIONAL GUY. I CAN'T BE WHAT SHE WANTS ME TO BE."

This is a big one. I used to think that because I wasn't wired to be super emotional or expressive, I'd never be able to give my wife what she needed.

But here's what I got wrong: She wasn't asking me to be an

emotional wreck or a different man—she was asking me to be present.

Your wife doesn't need you to cry at rom-coms or have deep heart-to-hearts every night. What she needs is to feel like you're there, engaged, and emotionally available in the moments that matter.

Being an emotionally grounded man doesn't mean turning into someone you're not. It means learning to hold space for emotions (yours and hers) without running, fixing, or shutting down.

That's real strength.

**What to Do:** You don't have to be "naturally emotional." You just have to be present. Next time she's upset, instead of withdrawing, just say, *"I hear you. I'm here."* Sometimes, that's all she really needs.

## "YEAH, BUT IF SHE RESPECTED ME MORE, I'D BE MORE LOVING."

Ah, the classic "I'll give when she gives" trap.

I believed this one for years. *"If she just respected me more, then I'd feel safe to be more affectionate, more open, more caring."*

Here's what I eventually had to face: Respect and love aren't transactions—they're responses to leadership.

Waiting for her to respect you before you step up and lead is like saying, *"I'll start rowing this boat once we reach the shore."*

If you want more respect, become a man worthy of it—no matter what she does. If you want more love, lead in a way that inspires it.

**What to Do:** Instead of focusing on what she's not giving, ask, *"What kind of man would inspire the love and respect I want?"* Then, become him.

## "YEAH, BUT NOTHING CHANGES NO MATTER WHAT I DO. I'VE ALREADY TRIED EVERYTHING."

I get it. You're exhausted. You've tried changing, apologizing, adjusting, and yet it feels like you're still hitting a brick wall.

But here's the uncomfortable truth: Have you actually tried everything, or have you only tried things on your terms?

For a long time, I thought I was doing everything I could to fix my marriage. But what I was really doing was repeating the same strategies that made sense to me—and getting frustrated when they didn't work.

True leadership means being willing to step outside your comfort zone and try things you haven't done before.

**What to Do:** Instead of saying, *"I've tried everything,"* ask, *"Have I actually led differently or just tried harder at the same things?"* Leadership isn't about effort—it's about strategy.


## "YEAH, BUT SHE'S JUST CRAZY EMOTIONAL. I CAN'T WIN."

I get it—sometimes it feels like no matter what you do, she's going to react emotionally. You say one thing the wrong way, and suddenly, you're in an argument you never saw coming.

But here's the truth I had to face: Her emotions aren't the problem—my response to them was.

See, when a woman is emotional, a lot of men think:

- *"She's being irrational."*
- *"This makes no sense."*
- *"I need to explain why she's overreacting."*

But that kind of thinking instantly puts you in opposition to her.

Your wife isn't looking for logic when she's upset—she's looking for connection. She wants to know if she can trust you to hold steady when she's feeling overwhelmed.

When I stopped trying to debate her emotions and started just being present for them, everything shifted.

**What to Do:** Next time she's upset, instead of thinking, *"Here we go again,"* try saying, *"I see you're really feeling something big right now. I'm here. Let's talk."* That's leadership.

## "YEAH, BUT I'M NOT RESPONSIBLE FOR HER FEELINGS. SHE SHOULD CONTROL HER OWN EMOTIONS."

This was a tough one for me because I used to think that if I wasn't outright hurting her, then her emotions were her problem, not mine.

But here's the distinction I missed:

- I'm not responsible for her emotions.
- But I am responsible for how I show up when she has them.

When I used to get defensive and say things like, *"That's your problem, not mine,"* it didn't make her less emotional—it made her feel more alone. And when a woman feels alone in a relationship, she stops trusting you emotionally.

Once I realized that I could be a stabilizing force rather than a dismissive one, the whole dynamic changed.

**What to Do:** Instead of thinking, *"Her emotions aren't my problem,"* ask, *"How can I be a man who makes her feel emotionally safe?"*

## "YEAH, BUT SHE'S THE ONE WHO BROKE TRUST. WHY SHOULD I BE THE ONE LEADING?"

I get it. Maybe she's the one who hurt you first. Maybe she lied, betrayed you, or did something that shattered your sense of safety.

So why should you be the one to lead?

Because you have a choice—stay stuck in blame or lead yourself into a better future.

If you're here reading this book, you don't want to stay stuck. You don't want to be the guy who lets bitterness win. And the hard truth? Even if she was the one who broke trust, healing won't happen by waiting for her to fix it alone.

I've coached men who have been deeply hurt. The ones who rebuild strong, thriving marriages are the ones who say, "I'm going to lead toward healing, even if she *broke things first.*"

**What to Do:** Instead of waiting for her to fix things, ask yourself,

*"What kind of man do I need to become to create trust again—whether with her or in my own life?"*

## "YEAH, BUT I SHOULDN'T HAVE TO DO ALL THIS JUST TO GET A LITTLE LOVE AND RESPECT."

I used to think this way, too. *"Shouldn't love and respect just be there? Why do I have to work so hard for something that should be natural?"*

Here's what I eventually had to accept:

- A great marriage isn't something you deserve—it's something you create.
- Love and respect aren't rewards for effort—they're responses to leadership.

The moment I shifted my mindset from "Why should I have to do this?" to "Who do I need to be to create the marriage I want?"—everything changed.

**What to Do:** Stop focusing on what feels unfair. Ask yourself, *"What if the life and marriage I want is on the other side of me stepping up?"*

## "YEAH, BUT IF I START DOING THIS, WON'T I BE ACTING LIKE A PUSHOVER?"

I understand why you might think that. Many men assume that being more emotionally present or leading with love means becoming weak.

But here's what you need to know:

- Strength isn't about resisting emotions—it's about handling them well.
- Leading with love doesn't mean rolling over—it means standing firm in who you are.

The men who think emotional leadership makes them "weak" are usually the ones who feel out of control when emotions come up.

Real strength is being able to stay calm, grounded, and unshakable—even when emotions get big.

**What to Do:** Instead of thinking, *"This makes me weak,"* ask, *"How does a truly strong man handle conflict and emotions?"* (Hint: It's not by shutting down or lashing out.)


## "YEAH, BUT WHAT IF I DO ALL THIS AND SHE STILL DOESN'T CHANGE?"

This is a real fear. You might be thinking, *"I don't want to put in all this effort if she's just going to stay the same."*

Here's the deal: You don't lead to force an outcome—you lead because it's who you choose to be.

When I started leading in my marriage, I had to let go of the need for immediate results. I had to say, *"Even if nothing changes right away, I'm still going to be the kind of man I'm proud of."*

And here's what I found: when I changed, the relationship changed—not instantly, but inevitably.

**What to Do:** Lead for you. Lead because it makes you a better man. And trust that when you shift, your marriage will shift, too.


## "YEAH, BUT MY SITUATION IS DIFFERENT. THIS WON'T WORK FOR ME."

Every man thinks his situation is unique. And in some ways, it is. But here's the thing—human dynamics are universal.

I've worked with men from all walks of life, and the core truth is the same:

- When a man steps into his strength, his marriage shifts.
- When he leads with calm, confidence, and presence, his wife responds.

Your situation might be uniquely painful, but the solution is the same: You must lead the way forward.

**What to Do:** Instead of thinking, *"This won't work for me,"* ask, *"What would it look like if I actually tried this with full commitment?"*

## "YEAH, BUT I SHOULDN'T HAVE TO BE PERFECT ALL THE TIME JUST TO HAVE A GOOD MARRIAGE."

Agreed. Perfection isn't the goal—presence is.

Your wife doesn't need you to be flawless. She just needs to trust that you're emotionally steady, engaged, and willing to grow.

**What to Do:** Forget perfection. Focus on consistency and presence.

## "YEAH, BUT I WORK HARD, I PROVIDE, AND I DO EVERYTHING I'M SUPPOSED TO. ISN'T THAT ENOUGH?"

Providing is great. But a paycheck isn't presence.

Many men believe that if they work hard, pay the bills, and stay committed, that should be enough. And in a way, it makes sense—most of us were taught that a man's primary duty is to provide and protect. But here's the hard truth: your wife doesn't just need financial security; she needs emotional connection. If you're doing all the right things on paper but missing the emotional piece, she will still feel disconnected.

You might be thinking, *"But I'm exhausted from working hard all day. How much more does she need?"* The answer isn't about doing more—it's about shifting how you show up. You don't have to spend every waking moment having deep emotional talks or constantly catering to her feelings. But you do have to be present—not just physically, but emotionally.

- Are you engaged when you're home or just zoning out on your phone or TV?
- Do you listen when she talks, or do you just nod and wait for the conversation to end?
- Do you make space for real connection, or do you assume your job is done once the bills are paid?

Being a provider is honorable. But if you treat your wife like another obligation instead of a woman who craves connection, she will feel alone—even with you right there.

**What to Do:** Ask yourself, *"Am I just providing, or am I actually present?"* Start by giving her your undivided attention for even 10 minutes a day—no distractions, no problem-solving, just presence.

## "YEAH, BUT WHY SHOULD I HAVE TO CHANGE? SHOULDN'T SHE LOVE ME AS I AM?"

Love isn't about staying the same—it's about growing together.

This is one of the biggest self-sabotaging beliefs men hold: *"If she really loved me, she wouldn't ask me to change."* But think about it— have you stayed exactly the same in every other area of life? Probably not. You've grown in your career, developed new skills, and adapted to new challenges.

Relationships are no different. A marriage that doesn't evolve is a marriage that dies.

This isn't about changing who you are at your core. It's about refining how you show up so you can lead more effectively. If your wife is asking for more connection, more presence, or more leadership, it's not because she wants to control you—it's because she wants to feel safe, seen, and deeply connected to the man she chose.

- Would you expect your career to thrive if you refused to grow in your skills?
- Would you expect your body to stay strong if you never adapted your training?
- Then why would your relationship thrive if you stay stagnant?

This isn't about losing yourself to please her. It's about becoming a more present, grounded, and intentional version of yourself—the man you actually want to be.

**What to Do:** Stop focusing on *"Why should I have to change?"* and start asking, *"Who do I want to become?"* Because when you step into growth, leadership, and confidence, she naturally responds with respect, trust, and attraction.

## MAIN TAKEAWAY: YOUR OBJECTIONS ARE THE LOCKS ON THE DOORS—BUT YOU HOLD THE KEY

Every "Yeah, but..." you've had while reading this book is a reflection of the very patterns that have kept you stuck. Those objections aren't just logical concerns—they're the defenses your mind has built to avoid the discomfort of change. But here's the truth: Every single man who has ever transformed his marriage and his life had the same doubts you do right now.

The difference? They didn't let their objections stop them.

The men who win in their relationships aren't the ones who never had doubts—they're the ones who chose to move forward anyway. They stopped waiting for proof, stopped arguing for their limitations, and started taking action before they felt ready.

So the real question isn't, "Yeah, but does this really work?"

The real question is: Are you willing to be the kind of man who finds out?

## UP NEXT: THE DEEPER WORK—WHY UNDERSTANDING ALONE ISN'T ENOUGH

At this point, you might think you have all the knowledge you need to change your marriage.

But if knowledge alone was enough, you wouldn't be here in the first place.

The truth is, your marriage struggles aren't just about what you didn't understand before reading this book. They're about what's been running beneath the surface—fear and judgment—two forces that have shaped the way you've shown up in your relationship (and your life) for years.

In the next chapter, we're going deeper.

Because real transformation isn't just about learning new ideas.

It's about dismantling the things that have been holding you back.

## FOURTEEN
# THE WORK ISN'T JUST ABOUT YOUR MARRIAGE

### IT'S ABOUT YOU

---

*Until you make the unconscious conscious, it will direct your life, and you will call it fate.*

— Carl Jung

---

## UNDERSTANDING ISN'T ENOUGH—WHAT'S REALLY HOLDING YOU BACK

If you've made it this far, you already see marriage differently than when you started. You understand why rooms close, why your wife brings up the past, and how to step into emotional spaces with confidence instead of fear.

But here's the truth men don't often want to admit:

Understanding alone doesn't change anything.

If simply knowing what to do was enough, you wouldn't be here. You wouldn't be looking for answers. And most importantly—you wouldn't keep running into the same struggles, even after gaining new insight.

Because the real problem isn't just a lack of understanding.

It's the presence of two deep-rooted forces that quietly undermine you at every turn:

- **Fear**—The silent force keeping you from taking real action.
- **Judgment**—The invisible weight keeping you trapped in the same patterns.

These two forces don't just affect your marriage. They affect your entire life.

And if you don't address them, no book, strategy, or framework —no matter how good—will truly change you.

## FEAR: THE HIDDEN DRIVER BEHIND EVERY HESITATION

Most men I meet don't consider themselves as fearful.

They think:

- "I'm not scared. I just don't want to screw things up."
- "I'm just trying to be smart about this."
- "I don't want to rock the boat and make things worse."

But that's just fear wearing a different mask.

- Fear of failure keeps you from taking decisive action.
- Fear of rejection keeps you from showing up fully in your marriage.
- Fear of discomfort keeps you from stepping into emotional conversations.
- Fear of looking weak keeps you from asking for help.

Fear doesn't always look like panic or paralysis.

Most of the time, it looks like hesitation, avoidance, and half-measures.

## JUDGMENT: THE POISON THAT TURNS STRENGTH INTO WEAKNESS

Judgment is what makes fear stick.

It's what turns a normal human emotion into a source of shame, keeping you locked in cycles of self-sabotage.

- You judge yourself for feeling fear, so instead of addressing it, you bury it.
- You judge your wife for being emotional, so instead of responding with strength, you shut down.
- You judge other men for needing help, so instead of seeking guidance, you convince yourself you should be able to figure this out alone.

Judgment is the voice that whispers:

*"You should be better than this."*

*"If you were a real man, you wouldn't struggle with this."*

*"Other men have this figured out—why can't you?"*

And that voice? It's a liar.

It keeps you trapped, pretending you're fine while slowly sinking under the weight of unaddressed fear, shame, and insecurity.

## HOW I DISCOVERED THIS—AND WHY I HAD TO FACE IT

I used to think I had all the answers.

I was successful, driven, and determined to figure things out on my own. I read books, studied psychology, and analyzed relationships like a problem to be solved.

But despite everything I "knew," I kept hitting the same walls.

- I was doing all the right things, but something still felt off in my marriage.
- I understood what my wife needed, but I still found myself withdrawing or getting defensive.
- I told myself I was leading, but deep down, I knew I was still avoiding the things that scared me most.

It took me years to realize that my problem wasn't a lack of knowledge.

It was fear and judgment running in the background, controlling my actions without me even realizing it.

I was afraid of rejection.

Afraid of looking weak.

Afraid of failing.

And I judged myself so harshly for these fears that I refused to admit them—burying them under layers of performance and logic and pretending to have it all together.

And until I faced those things head-on, nothing really changed.

The moment I stopped pretending I had all the answers...

The moment I stopped running from my own fears...

The moment I stopped judging myself for struggling...

That's when everything shifted.

Not just in my marriage—but in my entire life.

## THE NEED TO GO DEEPER

If you're serious about not just improving your marriage—but becoming the kind of man who thrives in every area of life—then you can't stop here.

You have to go deeper.

- Deeper into the fears you've been avoiding.
- Deeper into the judgments you've placed on yourself and others.
- Deeper into the kind of personal transformation that doesn't just change your relationship—but changes you.

Because this journey isn't just about learning how to communicate better with your wife.

It's about becoming the kind of man who moves through life with unshakable confidence, clarity, and purpose.

And that's not a quick process.

It's not something you fix in one book, one conversation, or one breakthrough moment.

It's a path—a path of mastery, growth, and surrounding yourself with the right men who push you forward.

That's exactly what we'll talk about next.

Because you can't do this alone.

## UP NEXT: YOU CAN'T DO THIS ALONE – BROTHERHOOD IS ESSENTIAL

Now that you see why deeper personal transformation is necessary, the next step is understanding why no man succeeds on this journey alone.

Because the biggest mistake men make is believing they can power through this by themselves.

And if you've ever wondered why some men seem to make massive, lasting change while others stay stuck in the same cycles for years—you're about to find out why.

Let's move forward.

# FIFTEEN
# THE RESILIENT HUSBAND
# PUNCH LIST
## THE HARD TRUTH OF WHAT KEEPS US
## WEAK, STUCK, AND UNATTRACTIVE

## GET RID OF THIS GARBAGE (OR STAY STUCK)

These are the poisons that sabotage your leadership, kill attraction, and keep your marriage in a cycle of conflict and distance. If you don't get rid of them, they will destroy trust, connection, and respect—both from your wife and from yourself.

If you don't kill these off, they will kill you off—and your connection.

### Toxic Mindsets That Keep You Weakened & Stuck

- **Bitterness** – The quiet cancer that eats away at your ability to love and lead.
- **Contempt** – The belief that you're above your wife, making you impossible to respect.
- **Resentment** – The scoreboard mentality that turns marriage into a battle of debts.
- **Blame** – The victim's way of avoiding personal responsibility.

- **Judgment** – The silent, smug way you convince yourself you're the "right one."
- **Animosity** – The slow-burning hostility that makes emotional safety impossible.
- **Scorekeeping** – The exhausting habit of tallying up who's right and who's wrong.
- **Defensiveness** – The knee-jerk reaction that blocks connection and shuts down conversations.
- **Avoidance** – The fantasy that ignoring a problem makes it go away (it never does).
- **Self-Pity** – The victim mindset that repels respect and attraction.
- **Coldness & Aloofness** – The illusion of strength that's really just hiding.
- **Niceness Instead of Kindness** – Niceness avoids conflict. Kindness is honest and strong.
- **More Toxic Behaviors That Sabotage Your Leadership**
- **Passive Compliance** – Doing what she wants just to keep the peace instead of leading with strength.
- **Martyrdom** – Acting like a victim who does everything but never gets appreciated.
- **Neediness** – Looking to her for validation and self-worth instead of standing strong in yourself.
- **Emotional Numbness** – Shutting down and withdrawing instead of engaging with presence.
- **Control** – Trying to manipulate or force outcomes instead of leading with confidence.
- **Insecurity** – Seeking constant reassurance instead of being anchored in your own value.
- **Fear of Conflict** – Avoiding tough conversations instead of leaning into them with calm strength.
- **Perfectionism** – Thinking you have to be flawless to be loved and respected.
- **Self-Righteousness** – Always needing to be "the good guy" instead of owning your flaws.

- **Comparison with Other Men** – The only man you need to compare yourself to is the man you were yesterday. Everything else is just insecurity.
- **Lack of Warmth** – Mistaking cold distance for strength instead of bringing steady, open-hearted leadership.

These aren't just bad habits—they're toxins. And the longer they live inside you, the more they rot your marriage from the inside out. Burn them to the ground.

## REPLACE THEM WITH THIS (IF YOU WANT TO LEAD WITH STRENGTH)

The men who build strong, thriving marriages are the men who build these traits within themselves.

### Resilient Mindsets That Build Trust & Connection

- **Ownership** – Everything in my life is my responsibility. No excuses. No blame.
- **Humility** – I don't need to be right—I need to be effective.
- **Curiosity** – Her perspective is different, not wrong. I want to understand it.
- **Emotional Stability** – I don't let my reactions lead—I lead my reactions.
- **Presence** – I stay in the room, even when it's uncomfortable.
- **Acceptance** – She is who she is. I stop resisting reality and start leading in it.
- **Attunement** – I pay attention, not just to words, but to emotion and meaning.
- **Leadership** – I go first in setting the tone for peace, connection, and trust.
- **Consistency** – I don't prove myself once—I prove myself daily.
- **Resilience** – Hard conversations don't break me—they build me.

- **Kindness Over Niceness** – I don't avoid conflict to make things easy—I bring truth with warmth.
- **Warmth & Strength Together** – I bring both, not one or the other.
- **More Resilient Mindsets That Keep a Marriage Strong**
- **Decisiveness** – Making strong, thoughtful decisions instead of hesitating or avoiding.
- **Confidence** – Being secure in who you are without needing approval from your wife.
- **Patience** – Giving the relationship space to heal instead of demanding immediate results.
- **Emotional Availability** – Being open and engaged instead of distant and closed off.
- **Courage** – Facing hard truths and leading difficult conversations instead of avoiding them.
- **Integrity** – Living in alignment with your values, even when no one is watching.
- **Self-Respect** – Holding boundaries and valuing yourself without arrogance or resentment.
- **Initiative** – Taking action before you're asked, instead of waiting for permission.
- **Calm Strength** – Holding steady in tense moments instead of reacting emotionally.

## THE WAY WE LEAD OUR MARRIAGE IS A REFLECTION OF HOW WE LEAD OURSELVES

If you're stuck in cycles of blame, avoidance, or resentment, it's not because you're broken or a horrible person—it's because you're using ineffective tools.

No man is beyond growth. But growth only happens when we're willing to be honest with ourselves. I need to work at this as much as the next guy.

Take a look at these lists—not as a way to beat yourself up, but as a way to get clear:

- Where have I been showing up in ways that aren't serving me?
- What patterns have kept me stuck?
- Where can I step up, not just in my marriage, but in myself?

A **reactive man** clings to the first list, even when it's clearly not working.

A **resilient man** has the courage to face reality, let go of what's not serving him, and lead himself forward.

**We get to choose which man we'll be.**

**What do you choose?**

# SIXTEEN
# CONCLUSION
## THIS IS YOUR MOMENT

At this point, you know what needs to be done.

You've seen the patterns that keep men stuck—avoidance, defensiveness, reactivity, waiting for our wife to change first. You've seen how marriages slowly become battlegrounds, how distance creeps in, how trust erodes, and how love that was once effortless can start to feel like a struggle.

But you've also seen the way *forward*.

You've seen what happens when a man takes ownership—when he stops trying to fix, control, or blame and instead leads himself first. You've seen that the most powerful men in their marriages aren't the ones who force submission or demand respect—they're the ones who earn it by how they show up every day.

And if you take nothing else from this book, let it be this:

**Your marriage is a reflection of your relationship with yourself.**

It mirrors your emotional strength, your leadership, your confidence, and how well you navigate your own inner world. If you're not leading yourself well—if you're reactive, uncertain, or driven by fear—your marriage will reflect that back to you.

This isn't about fixing <u>her</u>.

It's about mastering <u>you</u>.

Because, at the end of the day, your life is not created by circumstances, luck, or catching a break.

It's created by the man you choose to become.

So don't just ask, "What do I need to do to fix this?"

Ask, "Who do I need to become to create the life I want?"

This isn't about perfection.

It's about stepping up when it would be easier to step back.

It's about standing strong when it would be easier to crumble.

It's about being unshakable in who you are, no matter how rough the road gets.

And here's the good news: You can do this.

No man reading this book is too far gone. No marriage is too broken. No pattern is so ingrained that it can't be changed.

But the men who win at this aren't the ones who just read about it. They're the ones who take what they've learned and act.

So what are you going to do?

Are you going to file this away as another book you read?

Or are you going to step into the mansion, open the doors, and lead?

Your wife isn't going to do this for you.

No one is coming to hand you leadership.

This is on you.

Not in a way that should feel heavy—but in a way that should feel freeing.

Because when you finally take ownership of yourself, when you stop waiting, when you become the man you were meant to be—everything changes.

Not in a day. Not in a week. But over time, through small, daily, consistent shifts that turn you into the kind of man your wife feels safe with, trusts, respects, and is drawn to again.

This is your moment.

The door is open.

The only question left is:

**Are you going to walk in?**

# AFTERWORD
## WALKING THE PATH TO RESILIENCY

Reading *The Resilient Husband* is one thing. Living it is another.

By now, we've walked through the locked rooms, the misunderstandings, and the hidden patterns that keep marriages stuck. We've seen what doesn't work, and we've seen what does. We've seen how trust is built, how connection is restored, and how leadership transforms everything.

But let's be honest—knowing the path and walking it are two different things.

And if you're like many men, you've felt a lot while reading this book.

Maybe some of it hit home in a way that inspired you—like a switch flipping on, giving you clarity about things that never made sense before.

Or maybe some of it frustrated you—like a gut punch, challenging your old ways of thinking, making you question things you once believed.

You might have felt:

- **Hope**—because now you see what's possible.

- **Excitement**—because you recognize the shifts that can change everything.
- **Relief**—because you realize you're not crazy, and you're not alone.
- **Conviction**—because some of this called you out in uncomfortable ways.
- **Defensiveness**—because parts of this may have felt unfair or hard to accept.
- **Frustration**—because you're seeing patterns you've been stuck in for years.
- **Overwhelm**—because it feels like there's a lot to change and like you have to be perfect to experience love.
- **Shame**—because it's easy to look back and regret how you've shown up before and the feeling that you just don't have what it takes.
- **Doubt**—because you wonder if you even have what it takes to lead this way.

Whatever emotions you felt—good or bad—they're a sign that this matters to you.

And here's something I've learned from years of working with men:

**How you respond to those emotions
will largely determine what happens next.**

Some men will use the concepts in this book to transform their marriages. Others will put it down and avoid thinking about it because facing the truth feels too uncomfortable.

That choice is yours.

But I'll tell you this—transformation isn't about being perfect. It's not about fixing everything overnight. And it's definitely not about beating yourself up.

It's about being willing to take an honest look at yourself without running away.

If some of what you read in this book stung a little, it's not because you're broken or failing as a man.

**It's because one voice within you knows what you are capable of and desires this strength,**
and another voice within you tells you it's *impossible*.

Those two voices exist in *every* man, like two wolves. Whichever one we feed is the one that will thrive and grow louder.

I know you want better for yourself and your marriage. That feeling—however uncomfortable—is the starting point for real change.

Many men have been duped into believing that discomfort means something is wrong and react to things that feel challenging or vulnerable with avoidance.

But that's a lie. That's what has probably gotten you the life you have now.

**Discomfort is not a stop sign.**
**It's an invitation to the life we yearn for.**

And if we only move forward when things feel easy, we don't move forward at all.

No one is coming to save you.

Not your wife. Not circumstances. And, Not luck.

It's on you to become the man who can create the life and marriage you want.

But here's the part some men will overlook:

**How you respond to the message in this book directly reflects the challenge you're facing in your marriage.**

## THE MIRROR IS SHOWING YOU SOMETHING—ARE YOU SEEING IT?

If this book made you feel defensive, misunderstood, or like you were being judged... brother, I need you to hear this:

I don't hold you in low regard. I don't think you're failing. And I do *not* think you're weak.

But I also know how it *feels* when someone holds up a mirror, and we don't like the reflection.

I know—because, for years, I blamed my wife (and employers, parents, friends, and circumstances) for how I felt inside.

I thought *she* didn't respect me. I thought *she* was ungrateful for everything I was doing. I thought *she* saw me as inadequate, unworthy, or not enough.

And that hurt.

But what I see now—what took me decades to understand—is that *she* wasn't actually the source of those feelings.

It was *me*.

I had a story inside me that was already there long before she ever said a word. And life—through my wife, my experiences and everything I resisted—kept showing me that story over and over again.

At first, I thought my wife was tearing me down. Now, she showed me precisely where I needed to heal. And I did, and now, I don't feel those things any longer, and we've not had an argument about the past in at least seven years.

In the same way, this book might be showing you something about yourself.

Not because I'm shaming you. I'm not. Not because I think you're failing. I don't. But because I refuse to lie to you and tell you that you're broken, hopeless, or powerless. You're not.

The problem isn't that I hold you in low regard.

The problem is that, deep down, **you might.**

And that, brother, is what I get up every day to help men overcome.

Because if that's true—if your emotional pain is coming from your own internal narrative—then why would you give me, or a book, or a wife, or anyone else such power over you?

## SO, WHAT NOW?

If you've made it this far, I applaud you. You didn't just skim through another relationship book—you dug in. You faced hard truths. You reflected on where you've been, where you are, and where you want to go. That takes grit. It takes courage. And it tells me one thing:

You're serious.

You're not just looking for more information. You're looking for transformation.

You want to lead your marriage with confidence.

You want to feel strong, solid, and unshakable.

You want to be the kind of man who builds something real and lasting.

And now, the choice is yours.

You don't need my permission to take the next step. You don't need anyone's permission. But if you've realized that trying to do this alone isn't working, then the next step is clear.

The doors are open. The path is in front of you.

Where you go from here is up to you.

# STEP INTO THE PATH OF RESILIENT MASTERY

## THE 21-DAY CHALLENGE & MASTERFUL MEN COMMUNITY.

*The strength of the pack is the wolf, and the strength of the wolf is the pack.*
— Rudyard Kipling

The doors are open. The path is in front of you. Now, it's time to take a step.

You've come this far, which means you're serious about leading your marriage with strength, presence, and resilience. You've seen the patterns that keep men stuck and the shifts that change everything. But understanding these concepts isn't enough—real transformation happens when you live them.

That's why I've created the **21-Day Resilient Husband Challenge**—so you can start applying these principles right now, in your daily life, instead of just thinking about them.

## THE 21-DAY RESILIENT HUSBAND CHALLENGE

To help you start living what you've learned in this book, I designed the **21-Day Resilient Husband Challenge**—a simple but powerful way to put these principles into action.

This challenge isn't just about checking boxes or completing assignments—it's about immersing yourself in an environment where real transformation happens.

## OPTION 1: THE 21-DAY CHALLENGE INSIDE MASTERFUL MEN

If you're serious about becoming a **Resilient Husband,** this is where it starts.

This challenge isn't some massive, impersonal group where you'll disappear into the background.

It's not another online forum where guys argue over theoretical ideas.

Frankly, this work isn't for everyone.

**Most men *aren't* ready for it.**

And because of that, what we have inside **Masterful Men** is something rare—an authentic, cohesive, and powerful community of leaders who are committed to mastering themselves and their relationships.

Inside the **21-Day Resilient Husband Challenge,** you'll get:

- **Authentic connection** with other men who are walking the same path.
- **Daily action steps and deeper exercises** that bring the book's concepts to life.
- **Live discussions, Q&A, and coaching** from me and other men actively walking this journey.
- **Real-world guidance** on your toughest relationship and personal challenges.
- **Accountability and encouragement** so you're not just reading—you're actually transforming.

This *isn't* just about becoming a better husband. It's about becoming men who lead our lives, our relationships, and ourselves with confidence, strength, and clarity.

And here's the kicker:

The cost of this challenge and community is *less than a large coffee every day.*

It's infinitely less than the cost of a failed marriage, a divided family, or years of frustration and resentment.

And the highest cost?

**The cost of doing nothing.**

If we keep doing what we've always done, we'll keep getting what we've always gotten.

If you're ready to actually live this out—not just think about it—**join us inside Masterful Men.**

🔗 **Go to www.ResilientHusbandBook.com to join.**

## OPTION 2: THE FREE 21-DAY EMAIL CHALLENGE

If you're not quite ready to step into the community, that's okay.

You can start small by signing up for the free **21-Day Resilient Husband Email Challenge** at **www.ResilientHusbandBook.com.**

Each day for three weeks, you'll receive a short but powerful action step—something simple you can apply immediately to shift your approach, deepen your connection with your wife, and lead your marriage with confidence.

This isn't as immersive or effective as the community, but it will help you start building momentum in just a few minutes a day.

## WHY MASTERFUL MEN?

Most men don't struggle because we lack intelligence, effort, or good intentions.

We struggle because we've never had a **real blueprint** for self-mastery, leadership, and emotional strength.

And that's exactly why this community is called **Masterful Men** —not because we're chasing some elitist ideal or trying to live above others, but because we are committed to **inner mastery.**

Being *masterful* isn't about controlling others, proving our worth, or demanding respect. It's about mastering ourselves—our emotions, our choices, our responses, and our ability to create the life and relationships we truly want.

A **Masterful Man** is:

- **Unstuck**—no longer trapped in cycles of fear, blame, or emotional reactivity.
- **Unshakable**—solid and stable, no matter what life or relationships throw at him.
- **Unstoppable**—a man who trusts himself fully, leads his life with confidence, and builds something meaningful.

This level of mastery begins with **unconditional self-acceptance.** The kind of self-acceptance that frees us from insecurity, shame, and dependency on external validation. It's the foundation that empowers us to create any life we desire.

Inside Masterful Men, we go far beyond just fixing relationships.

- We learn how to become unstuck, unshakable, and unstoppable—emotionally solid, self-led, resilient, and confident in who we are.
- We break free from old patterns of shame, anxiety, fear, judgment, dependency, reactivity, and frustration.
- We get the tools to lead our marriage, family, and life with clarity and strength.
- And most importantly—we do it alongside other men who are just as committed as we are.

Because if we want a thriving marriage, we need to be surrounded by thriving men.

Men who challenge us, encourage us, and won't let us shrink into old patterns.

This is where we become the kind of men we were always meant to be.

This is where we finally learn the things we wished our dads had taught us.

This is where we learn how to be the kind of men who lead, love, and build something meaningful.

## THIS ISN'T THE ONLY PATH—BUT YOU NEED *A* PATH

I'm not here to tell you that *Masterful Men* is the only way. It's not.

There are many ways to step into growth, leadership, and resilience as a man, and I don't have a corner on that. The most important thing *isn't* that you join what I offer—it's that you **take personal action.**

I created *Masterful Men* because I saw a need—for myself, and for the many men I've worked with. I built what I wished had existed when I was stuck. But if you find another path that works for you, take it.

Just don't do what many men will do—read this book, feel inspired, and then do nothing.

## WHICH PATH WILL YOU CHOOSE?

You've read the book. You've seen the map.

Now it's time to walk the path.

Join us inside Masterful Men and take the 21-Day Resilient Husband Challenge with real support, guidance, and accountability.

If you're not ready for that yet, at least start the free email challenge—but know that at some point, you will need other men beside you on this journey.

Either way, your next 21 days could change everything.

Get started at www.ResilientHusbandBook.com today.

# ABOUT SVEN MASTERSON
## & HOW TO CONNECT

Sven Masterson is an author, men's coach, mentor, and the founder of Masterful Men, a global community dedicated to helping men become **unstuck, unshakable, and unstoppable**—even in the face of life's greatest "alien invasions." Specializing in guiding men through high-conflict relationships, Sven helps men uncover and resolve the root issues that sabotage connection, intimacy, and trust in their partnerships.

Drawing on over thirty years of marriage, parenting, and entrepreneurial experience, Sven offers relatable and authentic guidance to men wrestling with frustration, resentment, or feelings of disconnection. His work provides actionable steps to rebuild confidence, emotional resilience, and connection—not just in relationships but in life as a whole. Whether working one-on-one, in small groups, or through his private community, Sven creates a safe, down-to-earth space where men can untangle their struggles, confront their fears, and step into strength and purpose.

Sven's coaching combines warmth, humor, and accountability to help men break cycles of conflict and self-doubt, confront issues like low self-worth, and move toward thriving relationships and lives. He believes in "facing your inner aliens head-on"—taking personal responsibility for growth and living with bold authenticity.

As a seasoned author, coach, and mentor, Sven has helped countless men navigate life's "invasions," equipping them with the tools to transform personal crises into opportunities for connection and growth. His work reminds men of what's possible when they show up for themselves, their partners, and their families.

Outside of his professional life, Sven enjoys outdoor adventures, travel, creating things, and exploring nature. He finds fulfillment in self-reliance pursuits like homesteading, gardening, cultivating and animals, and hands-on crafting, reflecting his commitment to living intentionally. He and his wife of thirty years, Zelda, live on a homestead in North Central Pennsylvania with three of their six children. There, they embrace the beauty and simplicity of rural life while always keeping an eye on the sky.

---

facebook.com/MentorSven

x.com/masterfulmen

instagram.com/masterful.men

linkedin.com/in/svenmasterson

amazon.com/stores/Sven-Masterson/author/B0D3YFWY5P

youtube.com/@SvenMasterson

# ACKNOWLEDGMENTS

To my Creator, the source of all wisdom, strength, and life—your unwavering presence has been my foundation. You remind me of who I am when I forget, and you continue to lead me toward freedom, love, and truth. To Yeshua, who embodies grace, power, and the courage to walk in both—I strive daily to follow your example.

To Zelda and our children—thank you for your love, patience, and resilience. You've been my greatest teachers, even when the lessons were hard-earned. Zelda, your strength and commitment to us, even when I didn't always make it easy, have shaped me in ways I can never fully express. This book is as much yours as it is mine.

To my parents, who instilled in me a relentless curiosity and a deep respect for truth. Dad, your quiet steadiness and kindness toward others gave me a blueprint for integrity. Mom, your intensity, passion, and hunger for understanding have fueled my own. To my sisters, who unknowingly prepared me for a lifetime of learning about the feminine—you taught me more than I realized at the time. And to my brother, my first challenger and partner in mischief, whose wit, humor, and ability to make me laugh at the absurdities of life have been a constant, welcome reprieve.

To my mentors, Steve Horsmon and Uncle Ed, thank you for challenging me to fully embrace my strengths and for showing me what it means to lead with clarity, confidence, and love. To Rob Schneps, your insights into judgment and the nature of the human struggle opened a new way of seeing, thinking, and living that profoundly shaped this work.

To my brothers and clients in the Masterful Men community, you have sharpened, challenged, and supported me in ways I never expected. Your willingness to step into the fire of growth, embrace discomfort, and pursue mastery with courage and camaraderie has been one of the most rewarding experiences of my life. Thank you for the adventure, honesty, laughter, and connection.

This book exists because of all of you. Thank you.

# ALSO BY SVEN MASTERSON

### FROM RESENTMENT TO RECONNECTION: A MAN'S GUIDE TO OVERCOMING PERSONAL AND MARITAL CONFLICT

Are you feeling stuck in cycles of resentment and disconnection in your marriage? This transformative guide offers practical steps to rebuild intimacy, trust, and emotional connection. Learn how to embrace high regard, self-reliance, and ownership to reignite love and partnership. More Info at ResentmentToReconnection.com

### NARCISSIST! OR NOT?: A MAN'S GUIDE TO TRANSFORMING HURTFUL ACCUSATIONS INTO LASTING LOVE & TRUST

Have you been called a narcissist? This book challenges harmful labels and provides tools to break free from cycles of defensiveness and conflict. Discover how to cultivate emotional strength, rebuild trust, and create deeper connection in your relationships. More Info at NarcissistOrNot.com

### WHAT TO DO WHEN THE ALIENS SHOW UP (AND EVEN IF THEY DON'T): A PRACTICAL GUIDE TO OVERCOMING FEAR, NAVIGATING UNCERTAINTY, AND THRIVING IN ANY CRISIS

Feeling overwhelmed by today's chaotic world? Whether you're facing personal struggles, societal upheaval, or even the possibility of extraterrestrial visitors, this book equips you with the tools to overcome fear, resist manipulation, and thrive in any crisis. Learn how to reclaim your personal power, build resilience, and navigate uncertainty with confidence and clarity. More Info at AlienArrivalBook.com

# A NOTE TO READERS
## A PERSONAL NOTE FROM ME TO YOU

Thank you for walking through this journey with me. If you've made it this far, it means you care deeply about your marriage, your leadership, and the kind of man you want to be. That takes courage, and I respect that.

If this book has resonated with you—if it's helped you see your marriage in a new way or given you tools to navigate challenges—I would be truly grateful if you shared your thoughts in a review where you purchased it. Your voice helps other men find this book, men who might be searching for exactly what you've discovered here.

If this book has sparked a transformation, challenged old beliefs, or raised questions you'd like to explore further, please feel free to contact me at sven@svenmasterson.com.

Your growth matters. Your leadership matters. And the work you're doing in your marriage isn't just about you—it's about building a legacy of love, trust, and strength that lasts.

Keep leading. Keep showing up. Most importantly, keep being the man you trust yourself to be.

With respect and encouragement,

**Sven Masterson**

# ENDNOTES

## SUPPORTING REFERENCES

While this book is an original work built upon my own experiences, observations, and insights, the following sources may align with and reinforce some of the key concepts explored throughout. These references are provided for readers who want to dig deeper into these ideas, offering additional context, research, and perspectives.

Their inclusion is **not** a tacit endorsement of every idea or conclusion within them, nor does it imply that this book was derived from them. Rather, they serve as valuable supplementary reading for those who wish to expand their understanding of the themes presented here.

## CHAPTER 1: THE MANSION OF LOVE—WHY MARRIAGE CHANGES OVER TIME

The Power of Metaphor in Understanding Relationships

- Lakoff, George, and Mark Johnson. *Metaphors We Live By.* University of Chicago Press, 2003.
  - Explores how metaphors shape our understanding of life, relationships, and emotions—including why

powerful metaphors, like the "mansion of love," can help us better navigate marriage.

How Relationships Change Over Time

- Gottman, John M., and Nan Silver. *The Seven Principles for Making Marriage Work.* Harmony Books, 1999.
  - Examines the gradual shifts that occur in marriage and how small moments, when left unresolved, can create distance and disconnection.

How Men and Women Experience Progress Differently

- Lewis, Michael. *The Undoing Project.* W.W. Norton & Company, 2016.
  - Explores how cognitive biases shape decision-making and perception—insightful for understanding why men and women naturally approach progress differently in relationships.

- Real, Terrence. *Us: Getting Past You & Me to Build a More Loving Relationship.* Penguin Publishing Group, 2022.
  - Discusses how men often focus on achievement and forward motion, while women prioritize emotional resolution and completion—highlighting the different ways partners define progress.

## CHAPTER 2: THE HAUNTED HALLS OF MARRIAGE—WHY THE PAST KEEPS COMING BACK

Why the Past Feels Like It Never Goes Away

- Lerner, Harriet. *The Dance of Connection: How to Talk to Someone When You're Mad, Hurt, Scared, Frustrated, Insulted, Betrayed, or Desperate.* HarperCollins, 2001.

○ Explains why revisiting past issues isn't about punishment but about emotional resolution and repair.

Why Avoiding Difficult Conversations Makes Things Worse

- Perel, Esther. *Mating in Captivity: Unlocking Erotic Intelligence*. HarperCollins, 2006.
  ○ Explores how emotional avoidance in relationships creates long-term disconnection and how engaging with difficult emotions fosters deeper intimacy.
- Brown, Brené. *Dare to Lead*. Random House, 2018.
  ○ Discusses how vulnerability is necessary for leadership, including in marriage, and how avoiding difficult conversations weakens trust and connection.

When Men Get Called "Narcissist" for Responding Defensively

- Masterson, Sven, and Steve Horsmon. *Narcissist! Or Not?* Sven Masterson, LLC, 2024.
  ○ Examines why many men struggling in their marriages —especially when avoiding difficult emotional conversations—end up labeled as narcissistic by their partners. This book helps clarify the difference between true narcissism and common misinterpretations of male emotional withdrawal.

## CHAPTER 3: THE SILENT KILLERS OF CONNECTION

Why Small Moments Matter More Than Big Ones

- Gottman, John M. *The Science of Trust: Emotional Attunement for Couples*. W.W. Norton & Company, 2011.

The Emotional Weight of Unfinished Business

- Brown, Brené. *Daring Greatly*. Gotham Books, 2012.

## CHAPTER 4: THE HIDDEN COST OF JUDGMENT

How Judgment Affects Relationships

- Tannen, Deborah. *You Just Don't Understand: Women and Men in Conversation.* HarperCollins, 1990.
  - Explores how men and women communicate differently, often misinterpreting each other's words and intentions, leading to unnecessary conflict.
- Gottman, John, and Nan Silver. *The Seven Principles for Making Marriage Work.* Harmony Books, 1999.
  - Discusses how criticism and defensiveness (often fueled by judgment) are among the four most destructive behaviors in relationships.

Psychology of Judgment & Perception

- Haidt, Jonathan. *The Righteous Mind: Why Good People Are Divided by Politics and Religion.* Vintage, 2012.
  - Explains how our subconscious judgments shape the way we see others, reinforcing misunderstandings and deepening divisions.
- Tversky, Amos, and Daniel Kahneman. *Judgment Under Uncertainty: Heuristics and Biases.* Cambridge University Press, 1982.
  - A foundational study on cognitive biases, including how we form quick judgments and attach meaning based on limited information.

Polarity and Relationship Attraction

- Gray, John. *Men Are from Mars, Women Are from Venus.* HarperCollins, 1992.
  - Covers the fundamental emotional and psychological differences between men and women and how misunderstandings erode connection.

- David Deida. *The Way of the Superior Man*. Sounds True, 1997.
  - Discusses the natural polarity in relationships and how misjudging or misunderstanding differences weakens attraction.

## CHAPTER 5: MEN MOVE FORWARD. WOMEN LOOK BACK (IS THAT WHY YOU'RE STUCK?)

Why Men and Women Process Emotions Differently

- Gray, John. *Men Are from Mars, Women Are from Venus*. HarperCollins, 1992.

How Unprocessed Emotions Stay Active in the Nervous System

- Maté, Gabor. *When the Body Says No: The Cost of Hidden Stress*. Wiley, 2003.

## CHAPTER 6: YOU CAN'T FIX YOUR WIFE'S FEELINGS—SO STOP TRYING

Why Fixing Your Partner Doesn't Work

- Hendrix, Harville, and Helen Hunt. *Getting the Love You Want: A Guide for Couples*. St. Martin's Press, 2007.

The Power of Emotional Validation

- Fosha, Diana. *The Transforming Power of Affect*. Basic Books, 2000.

## CHAPTER 7: WHY MEN DREAD EMOTIONAL CONVERSATIONS

Why Emotional Conversations Feel Threatening to Men

- Cozolino, Louis. *The Neuroscience of Human Relationships: Attachment and the Developing Social Brain.* W.W. Norton & Company, 2014.

How to Stay Calm in Emotional Conversations

- Siegel, Daniel J. *Mindsight: The New Science of Personal Transformation.* Bantam, 2010.

## CHAPTER 8: SHE'S NOT SEARCHING FOR FLAWS—SHE'S ASKING IF SHE CAN TRUST YOU

The "Open Loop" Theory of Emotional Processing

- Levine, Peter A. *Waking the Tiger: Healing Trauma.* North Atlantic Books, 1997.

How Emotional Memory Works in Relationships

- Van der Kolk, Bessel. *The Body Keeps the Score: Brain, Mind, and Body in the Healing of Trauma.* Penguin, 2014.

## CHAPTER 9: YOU CAN'T LEAD HER IF YOU'RE EMOTIONALLY WEAK

Why Emotional Leadership Starts with Self-Regulation

- Goleman, Daniel. *Emotional Intelligence: Why It Can Matter More Than IQ.* Bantam, 1995.

The Power of Non-Reactivity in Relationships

- Tatkin, Stan. *Wired for Love.* New Harbinger Publications, 2011.

## CHAPTER 10: YOUR MARRIAGE IS BUILT IN THE BORING MOMENTS

Why Small Daily Actions Build Strong Relationships

- Finkel, Eli J. *The All-or-Nothing Marriage: How the Best Marriages Work*. Dutton, 2017.

The Science of Relationship Rituals

- Heath, Chip, and Dan Heath. *Switch: How to Change Things When Change Is Hard*. Crown Business, 2010.

## CHAPTER 11: SOME WOUNDS DON'T HEAL ON THEIR OWN

The Psychology of Betrayal and Rebuilding Trust

- Perel, Esther. *The State of Affairs: Rethinking Infidelity*. Harper, 2017.

Why Resentment Builds When Wounds Go Unaddressed

- Neff, Kristin, and Christopher Germer. *The Mindful Self-Compassion Workbook*. Guilford Press, 2018.

## CHAPTER 12: STOP PLAYING DEFENSE AND START LEADING

How to Build a Marriage That's Strong, Passionate, and Unshakable
How Couples Shift from Conflict to Connection

- Johnson, Sue. *Hold Me Tight: Seven Conversations for a Lifetime of Love*. Little, Brown Spark, 2008.
  - Introduces Emotionally Focused Therapy (EFT) and how secure emotional bonds create lasting intimacy.

Why Leadership and Love Go Hand-in-Hand

- Lewis, C.S. *The Four Loves*. Harcourt, 1960.
  - Explores the different forms of love and how they shape relationships, including the role of leadership in deep connection

The Power of Leading with Emotional Strength

- Willink, Jocko, and Leif Babin. *Extreme Ownership: How U.S. Navy SEALs Lead and Win*. St. Martin's Press, 2015.
  - Explains how leadership principles from the battlefield apply to personal relationships, particularly in taking responsibility for emotional growth.

## CHAPTER 13: THE "YEAH, BUT..." OBJECTIONS THAT KEEP MEN STUCK

How Resistance to Change Keeps Men Trapped

- Pressfield, Steven. *The War of Art: Break Through the Blocks and Win Your Inner Creative Battles*. Black Irish Entertainment, 2002.
  - Examines the role of resistance and self-sabotage in personal transformation, highlighting how internal objections keep men stuck in patterns of inaction.

The Science of Justification and Self-Deception

- Tavris, Carol, and Elliot Aronson. *Mistakes Were Made (But Not by Me): Why We Justify Foolish Beliefs, Bad Decisions, and Hurtful Acts*. Harcourt, 2007.
  - Explores how cognitive dissonance leads people to defend their actions instead of changing their behavior, a key factor in why men resist taking responsibility in relationships.

The Power of Taking Ownership

- Jocko Willink and Leif Babin. *Extreme Ownership: How U.S. Navy SEALs Lead and Win.* St. Martin's Press, 2015.
  - Emphasizes how true leadership starts with personal responsibility—owning one's role in problems instead of blaming external factors.

## CHAPTER 14: THE WORK IS'T JUST ABOUT YOUR MARRIAGE

The Role of Fear in Men's Emotional and Relationship Challenges

- Glover, Robert. *No More Mr. Nice Guy: A Proven Plan for Getting What You Want in Love, Sex, and Life.* Running Press, 2003.
  - Explores how fear of rejection, failure, and disapproval keeps men trapped in patterns of avoidance and emotional withdrawal.
- Brown, Brené. *Daring Greatly: How the Courage to Be Vulnerable Transforms the Way We Live, Love, Parent, and Lead.* Avery, 2012.
  - Discusses how fear of vulnerability prevents men from fully engaging in their relationships and personal growth.

Judgment, Shame, and the Internal Barriers to Change

- Kegan, Robert, and Lisa Laskow Lahey. *Immunity to Change: How to Overcome It and Unlock the Potential in Yourself and Your Organization.* Harvard Business Press, 2009.
  - Examines why even highly intelligent and self-aware people struggle to make real change, often due to unconscious fears and deep-seated self-judgment.
- Lewis, C.S. *The Screwtape Letters.* HarperOne, 2001 (originally published 1942).
  - Though fictional, offers insight into the internal voices

of doubt and judgment that keep men from taking action.

The Power of Self-Awareness in Overcoming Fear and Judgment

- Jung, Carl. *Man and His Symbols*. Dell, 1964.
  - Explores how making the unconscious conscious (as referenced in the chapter's opening quote) is key to personal transformation.
- Tolle, Eckhart. *The Power of Now: A Guide to Spiritual Enlightenment*. New World Library, 1999.
  - Discusses how awareness of fear and judgment in the present moment allows men to break free from old patterns.

## CHAPTER 15: YOU CAN'T DO THIS ALONE

Why You Can't Do This Alone and What It Takes to Truly Transform The Power of Brotherhood in Personal Growth

- Pressfield, Steven. *The Warrior Ethos*. Black Irish Entertainment, 2011.
  - Explores the necessity of camaraderie, discipline, and shared struggle in a man's journey to strength.

Why Long-Term Growth Requires Deep, Ongoing Work

- Clear, James. *Atomic Habits: An Easy & Proven Way to Build Good Habits & Break Bad Ones*. Avery, 2018.
  - Discusses how small, consistent habits—rather than dramatic efforts—lead to lasting transformation.

The Role of Fear and Judgment in Holding Men Back

- Tolle, Eckhart. *The Power of Now: A Guide to Spiritual Enlightenment*. New World Library, 1997.

- Examines how fear-based thinking and self-judgment keep men stuck, and how presence creates personal power.